NOT MUCH TIME
FOR THE
THIRD WORLD

ERHARD EPPLER

NOT MUCH TIME
FOR THE
THIRD WORLD

Translated from the German by
GERARD FINAN

OSWALD WOLFF

LONDON

© 1972 for the English edition by
OSWALD WOLFF (PUBLISHERS) LIMITED,
London W1M 6DR

First published in Germany in 1971 by
VERLAG W. KOHLHAMMER, under the title
Wenig Zeit für die Dritte Welt

ISBN 0 85496 221 2

MADE AND PRINTED IN GREAT BRITAIN BY
THE GARDEN CITY PRESS LIMITED
LETCHWORTH, HERTFORDSHIRE
SG6 1JS

Contents

5

Preface

This book is not the work of a researcher even though some of the literary material used in it is of a scientific nature. Nor is it the product of a government department, though I wish here to acknowledge the assistance I have received from officials of the Federal Ministry for Economic Co-operation, especially Gudrun Graichen-Drück, Lutz Bähr and Heinrich Dehn, who have given me valuable material, suggestions and criticism. It is rather the work of a politician whose aim is not only to analyse and help set out the facts clearly but to achieve a political effect. Its object is to present development policy as one of those areas in which the decision whether we are capable of mastering the future will be taken.

If the reader puts this book aside having gained the impression that the prospects of our doing so are none too favourable, he will not find me contradicting him. If after reading it he is somewhat confused and wants to learn more about this terribly complicated subject, he will have my every sympathy. If he is plagued with doubt as to whether some of the standards of our own society are still valid, he will have understood what I am trying to say. And if, in spite of everything, he is determined not to give up in despair but to do something about it, then the time I have devoted to this book at the expense of other work will have been worthwhile.

August 1971   ERHARD EPPLER

Decade of Violence?

EAST PAKISTAN, Bengal, Bangladesh—the mention of these regions conjures up pictures of horror for the European : the bloated bodies of children lying in the mud left behind by the receding floods, ricksha drivers lying shot dead in the streets of Dacca, the corpses of cholera victims. What, compared with this, do figures say which no one can picture? One hundred thousand dead—or were three times as many drowned, five times as many killed in the slaughter?

The reaction in Europe from one catastrophe to the next is more of resignation than of emotion. Is that perhaps a part of the world where human life is of less value, where all this kind of thing is a matter of course? Whatever the case may be, wherever the dead are seen lying in the streets, there is always a feeling of sympathy, whether it was hunger or Chinese ammunition that put an end to their lives. And where millions of people flee from their homelands and struggle in the refugee camps to survive the monsoon rains there is an upsurge of pity, but it is short-lived for, after all, it is merely a question of alleviating the misery and distress which has suddenly occurred.

In the case of East Bengal we will not seriously be able to persuade ourselves that all this happened by accident and will soon be gone again. Flooding occurs in other parts of the world, too, but people can protect themselves by building dykes or regulating the flow of rivers. Why not here?

Naturally, the first thing that will have to be done is to examine the political causes of the Bengal disaster. And it will be necessary to describe that mixture of

9

short-sighted demagogy, rigid nationalism and formal concepts of law and order which has thrown a whole subcontinent into a state of paralysis at the very moment when both Indians and Pakistanis have in free elections once more demonstrated their hope for a better future.

No, easy as it may be to place the blame on the eruption of political passions in Pakistan, there is precious little to support the argument that it all came about by accident. The need for a special aid programme for East Pakistan and Bengal had been discussed long before the catastrophe happened. Only, where was the money to come from? In the former East Pakistan 72 million people live in an area half as big as the Federal Republic of Germany, a population greater than that of the whole German Reich of 1937. Two-thirds of the country can be used for agriculture, but this area is cut back considerably by the annual floods and tidal waves. On average, there are 800—in many parts of the country more than 1,000—people to every square kilometre of cultivable land and the average annual income per head is about half the average monthly income in the Federal Republic of Germany. The population is growing at the rate of about 3 per cent every year, which means that the present figure will be doubled before the end of this century. There is little industry, the principal commodity being jute. In 1961 the labour force was 10 million and there were over 8 million jobless men. Little was done to improve infrastructure during the colonial era, and not much more later on, particularly as the deltas of the Ganges and other rivers present additional obstacles.

It was surely not by chance that the people of East Pakistan started to look for a scapegoat and thought they had found one in the shape of the central government in Rawalpindi. Nor was it all that incomprehensible that many expected of an independent Bangladesh something which probably no one can offer them : a better future. We can work out the time when 1,500 or even 2,000 people in that country will be wanting to live off one square kilometre of land, most of them doing agricultural work. And we also know that this is not on, even if they were to plant no more than rice from the Philippines and Mexican wheat.

Many millions, mostly Hindus, fled to the Indian part of Bengal, but there the situation is not much different. An area the size of Austria holds 48 million people, that again works out to about 800 per square kilometre, and another growth rate of more than three per cent. The capital of Bengal is Calcutta, perhaps the most intolerable example of overpopulation known to the world —at present some eight million. Into this Bengal streamed the refugees from East Pakistan. Even if their fear of West Pakistan troops had been unfounded, their fear of hunger was not, for the ships and the boats on East Pakistan's rivers were few and far between and the railway which accounted for 60 per cent of all transport was paralysed by the destruction of bridges. In the summer of 1971, 80 per cent of the region's industries had ceased production, the administration was no longer functioning, and no taxes were being levied.

In the meantime there has been further bloodshed, in the war between India and Pakistan. Nobody can justify war, but can we take offence at the words of the Indian who said that though war was always bad there were worse things for the Indian subcontinent? The misery of the refugees, overpopulation, hunger, disease, unemployment, but above all the despair—all this can reach a stage where the transition to naked violence no longer comes as a surprise to anybody. There are many vicious circles in the Third World—are the 1970s likely to add another : desperation leading to violence, violence disrupting and destroying development and thus producing even more desperation?

There are people of outstanding intelligence in the western world who are not too much disturbed by this. They feel that such catastrophes can be localised and do not affect the industrial nations. But apart from the fact that, as Georges Bernanos says, some things turn the stomach even if the conscience is not stirred, the calculation is far from sound. If the '70s turn out to be the decade of violence, Europe, too, will not remain an island of the blessed.

I Nothing Swings Back Into Line

1. DEVELOPMENT

Hardly any word passes more easily over the tongue than "development", irrespective of the type of system that uses it or of the part of the world involved. Erich Honecker, First Secretary of the East German Communist Party, used this word ninety-five times in his speech before the VIIth party congress.[1] Not only politicians would be reduced to a stammer if this word were suddenly banned. It is convenient, fits into nearly every context, sounds serious and a little optimistic.

This is because of its origin. As late as the 17th century, history was understood and taught as the succession of events, persons and anecdotes which could at best be given an allegorical interpretation or a moral censorship. It was not until the mid-18th century that history was seen as the growth, development, flourishing and decay of cultures and nations. It was then, in the works of Hamann and Herder, that the concept "development" was born. It gives expression to a new discovery, the realisation that history is not a mechanical process or string of individual facts, not a showcase of curiosities, but something which is analogous to the processes of nature, like a leaf developing from a bud.

To this mixture of romanticism and enlightenment has been added the liberal concept of equilibrium, that the interplay of the forces of evolution brings about and accelerates development. So, even though we may no longer be conscious of the fact, the word "development" embodies a view of history which did not take shape until 200 years ago. Inherent in development is the idea of the natural, the organic, the necessary, the rational, and no doubt of progress, of evolution. This is also true of the German word "Entwicklung" and the French "développement"[2]. Where this does not appear to be the case we speak of misdevelopment, a regrettable divergence from the normal, but at some time or other it will swing back into line—and this is part of the concept of development. When we speak of developing countries this term contains a larger element of ideology then we are prepared to admit. Every development has an objective, in their case probably the industrial society which we have created in many parts of the Northern hemisphere, and the plan is to move, to develop, towards it steadily, with as few jerks as possible. That is only natural, necessary, and therefore also sensible, but now it is slowly beginning to dawn upon us that the validity of these ideological premises could be questionable.

This begins with the objective itself. Nobody can imagine India, which by the turn of the century will probably have a population of 1,000 million, with 250 million cars on the road. That would be the case applying West European standards. At the moment India has half a million cars and these are enough to make the air in her cities intolerable. Naturally, India will industrialise herself, but an industrial society built on our 1970 model surely cannot be her aim. But still more doubts arise if we consider the approach to that objective. For most countries of the Third World the process we call development begins with events that have nothing to do with natural growth from their own beginnings : the destruction of all organic structures and social equilibrium. The best known example is the empire of the Incas. Here there was "a balance between man and cultivated land",[3] a well organised society with forms of social security, but before it had developed it fell victim to the *Conquista-*

dores. The situation elsewhere may have been less spectacular and social structures more primitive, but the intervention of the Europeans always began with the disruption of development, upsetting the balance and forcibly integrating the nation concerned into a world economic system, mostly in the clearly defined role of raw material supplier.

The result was the sometimes grotesque disparities between the old and the new, between indigenous and borrowed characteristics, between the "symptoms of constancy and of change",[4] which can confuse any visitor to Africa or Asia. A Gandhi with loincloth, the spinning wheel and the telephone were certainly not the symbols of an organic development but of a nation thrown off its own path of development and looking for a new way, of a sub-continent where social structures and institutions that have stood still clash with dynamic technological and economic developments. It is indeed a common feature of most developing countries that they were denied an organic growth of their own initiative and dynamism, that they are having to cope with conflicts among themselves that have ensued from the intervention of another civilisation, that they must laboriously seek a new dynamic balance (in some cases, even their identity) now that the old one—let us not take too idealistic a view of it—has been irrevocably destroyed.

How little this resembles development in the strict sense of the word is indicated by the dangerous shift in the balance between medical and technological progress. The European colonial ruler did not by any means bring all his accomplishments to the developing countries at the same time. The fight against epidemics and infectious diseases was successful in the Third World before any serious attempts were made to promote industrial development. The result has been what we today call the "population explosion", except that even this term fails to indicate to us the special nature of this development.

2. THE DIFFERENCE

Europe, too, has experienced rapid population growth over the past 150 years. In 1900, Great Britain had nearly four times as many inhabitants as in the year 1800, and in the territory of what is now the Federal Republic of Germany the population in 1914 was three times greater than a century before, and that in spite of the fact that millions emigrated. But the difference was that this rapid population growth, which was chiefly the result of the falling rate of infant mortality and a more or less constant birth rate in Europe, was accompanied by a dynamic process of industrialisation. The additional children from rural areas who remained alive ultimately found work in industry, usually a miserable existence, but nevertheless a productive one for the economy as a whole. Prosperity increased and social security ensured that children were no longer looked upon as a safeguard against insecurity in old age. Education became available to widening sections of the population, and during this century the birth rate has more or less equalled the lower mortality rate. Nearly all modern industrial states, including the Soviet Union and Japan, show the same S curve with regard to population growth : hardly any noticeable rise prior to the beginning of the first industrial revolution, then a steep climb followed by another levelling off after about three generations.

Of course, it could be pointed out that some Asian countries have already reached the crest of the S curve. In Singapore,[5] the population growth as late as 1960 was 3.4 per cent, but in 1965 it had dropped to 2.5 and in 1968 was down to 1.6 per cent. In Korea, the population increase in 1960 was 2.9 per cent, and in 1969 only 2.2 per cent. Through family planning Taiwan has also achieved amazing results. In 1955 and 1960 the growth rate was 3.7 per cent but in 1967 only 2.6 per cent— doubtless a success, but even 2.6 per cent is still a high rate of growth, above average for South East Asia (2.2

per cent). In most developing countries, however, the situation is different, the rate in recent years having tended to increase and in fact the 2.5 per cent average estimated for the '70s must already be revised upwards. There is no reason to assume that countries like Pakistan, Kenya or Equador will in the foreseeable future be able to register a levelling out of the population curve, not even if family planning is considerably intensified. Where the level of education cannot be raised, the number of unemployed increases rather than decreases, and where the standard of living can hardly improve, then neither can the birth rate fall—and where the birth rate cannot be reduced educational standards can be raised only with extreme difficulty, unemployment cannot be checked, and therefore living standards improve only slowly.

In Africa only 8.8 million children attended primary school in 1950, whereas the figure had risen to 27 million by 1966. In Latin America and Asia, too, the figure had more than doubled in 1966 as compared with 1950. All the same the primary school intake in many countries is only 50 per cent, and half of these leave before they have completed four years. The absolute number of illiterates increased between 1960 and 1970 from 740 to 810 million. According to an excellent study carried out by the International Labour Organisation, the number of jobs available in Columbia[5a] increased by 2.3 per cent a year between 1965 and 1970, but the number of people in or seeking employment grew by 3.2 per cent. This working population will increase from 6.5 million in 1970 to about 11 million in 1985 (the children who by then will be looking for work have already been born). If the present rate of growth continues, between 7 and 7.5 million jobs will be available in 1985, which means that between 3 and 4 million people will be out of work. And Columbia is a country with a relatively high rate of economic growth (5.6 per cent a year). There are countries where the struggle against unemployment will be considerably more uphill than in Columbia, if only because the limit between underemployment and unemployment is even harder to determine.

The OECD puts the average unemployment figure in developing countries at about 10 per cent. If one includes the "invisible" number of unemployed then all calculations come to at least 20 per cent. According to estimates made in September 1969 by a group of UN experts under Mr. Gunnar Myrdal, unemployment and underemployment at the end of the coming decade may easily account for half of the labour potential of the developing countries unless this problem is tackled as such.[6]

If one of the eminent researchers in this field, Fritz Baade, speaks of the idle reserves of prosperity and the goldmine[7] of the developing countries inherent in the millions of unemployed, when he recommends that the "hundreds of millions today employed in agriculture in the developing countries and showing practically no national product must be mobilised, in other words, they must be found work outside agriculture",[8] then anyone should be able to judge for himself the awesome gap between theoretical necessity and practical possibility.

The prospects in the food sector are a little more favourable. Certainly, the Green Revolution holds out fair prospects of food production in the developing countries being increased at a faster rate than population growth, but although in recent years it has been possible in all developing countries to produce more food, the rate in *per capita* terms has not improved, indeed in some cases it has deteriorated (infra Table I). Between 1965 and 1968, annual food production in Africa increased by 2.2 per cent, but in population terms it was down by 0.3 per cent. Latin America's production went up by 2.8 per cent but the *per capita* average decreased by 0.1 per cent. And with an annual growth of 2.6 and 2.2 per cent in the Far East and Middle East respectively, the *per capita* increase was just 0.1 per cent.

In some Latin American and African countries the

18

Table I : Individual Countries

Annual average between 1952 and 1956=100

1969	Food production	Per capita food production
Latin America	151	99
South America	148	98
Argentina	124	96
Brazil	180	91
Chile	131	91
Colombia	148	92
Paraguay	143	95
Peru	144	94
Venezuela	231	133
Nicaragua	158	98
Indonesia	137	97
Philippines	155	95
Syria	139	90
Africa	138	96
Dahomey	123	81
Guinea	136	88
Nigeria	127	81
Somalia	98	93
Congo, Dem. Rep.	146	70
Ghana	176	118
India	145	104
Pakistan	154	100

Source : FAO, Rome 1970 : The State of Food and Agriculture 1970, pp. 2, 232, 261, 262.

situation is much worse. If one takes 100 as the mean value for food production between 1952 and 1956, then Dahomey's production up to 1969 had increased to 123 points, but in terms of the population production was down to 81 points.

The position is similar in Colombia : production up to 148, the *per capita* amount down to 92. Most striking is the disproportion in Brazil : production increased to 180 but *per capita* distribution only 91. All the same, agricultural progress in the developing countries resulting from the advance of science and technology has reached the developing countries just in time. Today mass starvation is by no means inevitable.

The growth of the big cities in Europe was also a painful process. What the proletariat who streamed into the towns and cities from the land found in the way of accommodation can be read in the works of Engels or Toqueville. Nevertheless, the process of urbanisation in most developing countries is under a much less favourable omen. The population of Asia's cities increased by 86 million between 1900 and 1950. This was the size of the population in all the world's cities together in 1900, but the proportion of the city population to the population as a whole increased from only 2.1 to 7.5 per cent. If, as the United Nations assume, the rate of urbanisation remains constant until the turn of the century, the earth will have another 1,000 million new city inhabitants in thirty years' time, in other words there will be 10,000 cities each with 100,000 inhabitants, a good three-quarters of them in developing countries.

Everyone is aware of the problems facing town planners in Europe and North America. John Kenneth Galbraith's view is slowly gaining ground. "The city of today", he says, "is an unimaginably expensive business."[9] But most cities of the Third World are today not even in a position to offer their citizens a minimum of the services which we take for granted, not to mention work and housing. In developing countries urbanisation is taking place in regions which are often much more densely populated than Germany in the 19th century. Consequently, the cities—even if Baade's recommendation is not followed—must absorb far more people at a much faster rate. Thus urbanisation could very well lead to a further increase in slum areas without sanitation and roads, without sewage or waste removal facilities, areas where people unable to make a living on the land are plunged into a struggle for survival.

If asked the worrying question whether this could not give rise to revolutionary structural changes, my answer would be : possibly not even that but merely the dissolution of all traditional structures, an amorphous increase in human misery and criminality.

3. Consumer Society Without Anything To Consume?

I have not written all this to horrify the reader but merely to show that there can be no question of a country in this position developing from within itself naturally and sensibly and therefore sooner or later re-adjusting itself. Where undernourished, underemployed illiterates live in huts made of sticks, sacks and paper and have no other opportunity in life than to produce even more undernourished, underemployed illiterates in even more huts made of sticks, sacks and paper, then this is not development but something which we still do not have words to match.

Juggling with figures to determine how many people the earth can feed is of little help if the 3,800 million already living on this planet could themselves make life on earth unbearable if they were all to consume as much energy, produce as much waste and pollute as much air and water as the average American. H. R. Hulett, a bio-chemist of Stanford University's Medical Centre, says he has calculated that based on the "present agricultural and industrial system of the world at US levels of afflu-ence",[10] the globe would only be able to afford an exist-ence to 1,000 million people. In their book entitled *Population, Resources, Environment,* Paul and Anne Ehrlich reached the conclusion that "in the context of man's present patterns of behaviour and levels of tech-nology"[11] the earth is already overpopulated.

Be that as it may, human society is not a huge rabbit hutch in which every inhabitant patiently waits in his compartment for his fodder. Anyone wishing to comfort our children, who towards the end of their lives will have to share the earth with 10, 12 or 14 thousand million people, by drawing their attention to the amazing possibilities of food production is telling them only a small part of the truth. People live neither on bread nor on growth rates alone; they want to learn, to work, to have a roof over their heads, to be able to cope with disease, to breathe fresh air and drink clean water, and in the long run they do not see why they should be denied what others have.

Here we see a further distinction from what happened in Europe during the 19th century. When the German Empire was founded the German worker did not yearn for a radio, a television set or a car, nor to fly abroad, and not even to have Coca-Cola, simply because there were no such things. There is a difference whether you have to do without things you do not even know exist and those which we are daily encouraged to buy. And if there is anything that reaches the slums then it is the advertisement. I shall never forget the day I stood at the end of a street that ran straight through a particularly depressing area of a big South American city and read on a huge poster the comforting news that it was now cheaper to fly to Tokyo. This may be a particularly grotesque example, but even slogans maintaining that a certain washing powder washes whiter or that yet another new refrigerator model is waiting for its customers sound insulting to the many who can hardly afford to buy even curd soap. Life in a society of general want is more bearable than life in a consumer society that has nothing to consume. The tremendous gap between ever newly aroused expectations and the little money available again shows that this is anything but development.

Social tensions are to be found in any society, especially the more dynamic it is. It is seldom that adequate social and political structures already exist when new industry is established. Not only Socialists but also conservative Liberals complained at the turn of the century that the German Empire, an industrial state, was ruled by an upper crust of wealthy landowners. In countries where the initiative for changes in production comes from outside such tensions may be considerably more pronounced. The probability of achieving a balance without violence, an evolutionary change, appears to be considerably less in some developing countries then it has been in Western Europe over the past 150 years. Where, as in Latin America, there are no businessmen of the kind described by Max Weber who, in the Calvinist tradition, combined industry, a sense of enterprise and disregard for personal needs, a free market economy will produce different results than in Britain or Holland. And this is only one of many differences.

Whatever the one or the other of us in our country may wish, we should start from the knowledge that in the social sphere, too, continuous development is much less likely in many countries than the dramatic and sometimes forcible release of tension. Wherever we look we come to the same conclusion : in the Third World the white man has started something for which the term "development" is not an accurate description but a euphemism. The continuation of what was and what is does not by a long chalk add up to a future. Nothing swings back into line.

The realisation of this comes as a shock—not only with regard to the Third World, but here the implications are more dramatic than elsewhere. It will require a planned, purposeful, joint international intervention if this course is to be altered in time. The Third World has not much time left.

II Objectives

1. CATCHING UP?

THE FACT that, seen under this aspect, the term "development aid" tends to cloud rather than clear our vision of reality is obvious. Naturally, there is no point in trying to eliminate an internationally accepted term, but we should at least know that we use it—*faute de mieux*—even though it is more than questionable, for with most developing countries it is simply not a matter of supporting or accelerating a natural process of development but of seeking a new dynamic equilibrium to replace the social, economic and demographic balance that has been destroyed forever.

It is frequently said—and I have done so myself— that the aim of "development aid" should be to enable countries to "catch up", to reduce the gap between their and the industrial countries' *per capita* income. Is this realistic? The fact that in 1970 the real growth alone of *per capita* income in the Federal Republic of Germany was greater than the full *per capita* income of half of the earth's population may sound like toying with figures. The data provided by Kahn and Wiehner[12] no doubt carry more weight. Table II shows that *per capita* income in Europe in 1965 was about ten times greater than in Africa. In 1975 it will be over eleven times greater, in 1985 fourteen times, by the year 2,000 just under eighteen times and in 2020 more than twenty-five times. It shows the prospects for Asia to be better, but here, too, the ratio in the year 2000 will be less favourable than in 1965, and in 2020 it will be one to

Table II : GNP per head of the population
(in US dollars for 1965)

	1965	1975	1985	2000	2020
Africa	141	174	209	277	407
Asia	152	214	308	577	1,436
Europe*	1,369	1,976	2,867	5,055	10,730
Oceania†	2,000	2,510	3,080	4,310	6,600
North America	2,632	3,403	4,329	6,255	10,280
South America	375	413	496	695	1,112

* European OECD and Warsaw Pact countries, including the whole of the Soviet Union.
† Australia and New Zealand.

seven, and Latin America's ratio will be worse than in 1965.

There is good reason to treat such calculations with caution. I start from the assumption that economic growth rates in the industrial countries will decrease to the same degree that people come to realise what Gustav Heinemann expressed as follows : "The mere increase in economic growth rates . . . is not a worthwhile objective if it is achieved at the expense of our physical and spiritual health."[13]

As regards the developing countries, quite a number of uncertain factors remain, such as population growth. All the same, up to now only a few of them can be said to have made up some leeway or to be capable of doing so in the near future.[14] In the Third World, too, the biggest growth rates are in the areas with the highest level of industrialisation. The largest and most important developing countries, including India, Pakistan, Indonesia, nearly the whole of Africa and the larger part of Latin America, are not among them. Even if it proves possible to achieve the growth rate of 6 per cent of the gross national product as set out in the United Nations Strategy Document, where there is a population growth of about 2.7 per cent actual *per capita* income will be left at little more than 3 per cent. According to all the estimates, the *per capita* income in the industrial countries during the 1970s is expected to increase faster than in the developing countries.

But if around São Paulo or Mexico City it is possible to achieve the enormous growth rates that push the average up so high it will be of little use to the peasants in India or Morocco, or in North East Brazil. A. P. Thirwall has tried to calculate on the basis of fairly realistic assumptions and data when the countries of the Third World will have made up the leeway. The results are grotesque : Peru would be able to draw alongside the EEC in terms of *per capita* income in 359 years, whereas Pakistan would need 1,356 years Whether Pakistan will still exist in the year 3325 or so is an open question, but it seems certain to me that by that time progress will no longer be measured in terms of economic growth. If there are then still historians who dig up such calculations, they will be amused to discover how the people of one epoch quite unabashed projected into the distant future standards which did not exist three generations previously.

The idea of catching up is a logical consequence of "development aid". If it is merely a question of accelerating a more or less rational development towards a goal we have already achieved, then in fact it is a matter of catching up, of closing the gap. Then there is the erroneous analogy to the Marshall Plan. In reality the funds provided under the Plan were used to speed up a process which would in any case have been set in motion after World War II, and in the same direction. Western Europe has actually made up the leeway, and to that extent the Marshall Plan was development aid in the strict sense of the word. If, especially in the United States, it had been clear from the outset that the task to be accomplished in the Third World was a fundamentally different one, then the Americans—and not only they— would have been spared many of the disappointments reflected in foreign aid budget appropriations since the mid-sixties. Those who make closing the gap the aim of their development aid policy will constantly have their lack of success totted up for them. Here, too, we are faced with the puzzling fact that figures show us how the apparently most simple, the most plausible, and the most pragmatic objectives can also be the most illusory.

2. SELF-SUSTAINING GROWTH?

Is the concept of "self-sustaining growth" more realistic? It implies that every country must at some time reach the point from where on its economic growth can sustain itself, can continue on its own momentum, without needing any other means than the usual commercial and financial facilities.[15] What speaks in favour of this objective is that we know from experience that a tangible and continuous improvement in their own living conditions can mean more to the poor than the gap between their own and the standard of living of the rich. This is all the more so if such progress is the result of their own efforts.

In practice, however, the flaws in this concept become apparent. Small countries and parts of large countries (for instance, Panama and the state of São Paulo) in many cases show high rates of growth owing to the fact that their position when they started out was more favourable, and indeed they became so attractive that they even draw capital and skilled labour from the poorer regions. But there is no machinery to ensure that other regions can follow suit (e.g. North East Brazil). And the situation of those who lag behind is all the more difficult the later they begin. The world does not stand still for them and they miss the "connecting trains". After the initial success, the process of industrialisation is again held up in the rough wake of technological advance and competition in world markets. This is more or less what happened to Argentina, whose situation after World War II ought to have been adequate to ensure rapid growth under its own steam.

The decreasing share of world trade accruing to the developing countries, the concentration of their modest growth in a few regions, and their mounting indebtedness, are not an indication that many of them will soon have reached the point of take-off. In fact that point recedes into the distance like a fata morgana, and the arid stretch they have to make up is lengthening all the time. As long as the developing countries continue to have structural deficiencies and are too weak to hold their own in world markets, self-sustaining growth will for most of them remain wishful thinking. But if this purely economic objective cannot be achieved within the foreseeable future the people of those countries will hardly be prepared to make sacrifices indefinitely.

3. How Much Can the Environment Take?

Considering all this, the question remains unanswered whether the industrialisation of the developing countries on the European or the American model is at all possible. It is understandable that discussion of environmental problems in the Western industrial countries should arouse suspicion among politicians in the Southern hemisphere. Is this, perhaps, only a trick to divert attention from the problems confronting the countries of the Third World? Or a pretext even to block their way to prosperity so that the highly developed countries can enjoy it in still greater leisure? At all events one must admit that in Bombay or Lima they have more urgent problems to attend to than the question of car exhaust fumes or the long-term effects of spraying with D.D.T.

This in no way alters the fact that the developing countries already have their own environmental problems : soil erosion and the formation of steppe through indiscriminate timber felling in West Africa or in

Sumatra, the polluted air over São Paulo or the waters of the Hooghly that runs through Calcutta. In actual fact the developing countries could be particularly vulnerable precisely on account of their climatic conditions and the tremendous speed of urbanisation.

The ecological balance is more delicate in the tropics than in Europe. Experts such as those members of the Association of German Scientists engaged in research in the field of development and the environment have established that after the use of D.D.T. in the Ivory Coast the plague of mosquitoes grew worse because the birds had been killed off by the insecticide, whereas the mosquitoes developed resistant mutations. The faster the sequence of generations, the quicker the development of resistant organisms. The higher the temperature, the lower the oxygen content in the air and the greater the risk of pollution.

The air in Mexico City is more polluted than the air in Frankfurt. If you walk through the city for longer than half an hour your eyes will more than likely start watering. About one and a half hours further north by car hundreds of Indios built a canal in 1970 to irrigate their barren, dust-laden land with *agua negra*, the black water from the sewage issuing from the city. This water is at the same time probably a welcome fertiliser, but huge white flocks of foam floating on the surface show that when the area is ploughed for the first time it will also absorb the poisonous substances emitted by a modern city. This could very well lead to a new kind of vicious circle which is described by Paul and Anne Ehrlich as follows :

"As population grows so does industry, which pours into our water supplies a vast array of contaminants : lead, detergents, sulfuric acid, hydrofluoric acid, phenols, ethers, benzenes, ammonia, and so on. As population and industry grow, so does the need for increased agricultural production, which results in a heavier water-borne load of pesticides, herbicides, and nitrates. A result is the spread of pollution not just in streams, rivers, lakes, and along seashores, but also (and most seriously) in groundwater, where purification is almost impossible. With the spread of pollution goes the threat of epidemics of hepatitis and dysentery, and of poisoning by exotic chemicals."[16]

Even if this is the beginning rather than the end of serious research on the subject, one thing is certain: nobody knows how the financial resources of a developing country can suffice to lead vast areas out of a way of life reminiscent of Stone Age civilisations and at the same time cope with the dangerous consequences of modern industrialisation in densely populated areas. It is not unlikely that such agglomerations will absorb any additional growth for their own rehabilitation. The countries of the Third World will soon realise that it is unwise to offer themselves as "environment oases" to foreign industrial enterprises who find the laws of their own countries an impediment.

But the limits of the biosphere are surely narrower still. If it is true, for instance, that in twenty years' time the carbon dioxide content of the air will have increased by about 18 per cent through the combustion of mineral fuels, and if as a result the temperature on our planet increases, if only slightly, then we can work out for ourselves what would be bound to happen if in sixty years a trebled world population wanted to consume the energy required by the average American citizen today—provided, of course, that so much power were at all available, which is highly improbable. Even before the United Nations Conference on the Environment to be held in Stockholm in June 1972 supplies us with more exact information on this subject, we can say:

    1. If the so-called developing countries were to undergo a process of industrialisation strictly along European and American lines, then not only would the

earth's entire biological balance be in danger but life in a number of these countries themselves would be rendered unbearable—and probably earlier.

2. Of course, this cannot mean that the industrialisation of the Third World will have to be stopped or prevented, but no doubt that from the very outset technologies will have to be found which will counteract pollution or destruction of the environment.

3. This will have to be reflected in traffic planning (the car will certainly not have the same importance as in Europe), power supply (perhaps nuclear energy will, in spite of everything, bring fewer dangers than other sources of energy), in the methods of and the laws and conditions for industrialisation, which may seem costly at first but can in the long run save the billions which the industrial countries are today having to invest subsequently.

4. Where sacrifices and restrictions become necessary in the interest of all they should not be confined to one group of countries.

5. The industrial countries will very quickly have to realise that help for the Third World and environmental protection are not conflicting alternatives but rather two aspects of the effort we are required to make if we want to keep the space-ship Earth inhabitable. This calls for new forms of international relations.

4. REQUIREMENTS

If, therefore, catching up on the standards of living and production of the industrial countries is neither possible nor desirable for most developing countries, what can be the object of that process which we—for want of a better term—call development, and of that activity which we—for the same reason—refer to as development aid?

How can these countries, who have lost their old equilibrium, be helped along the road to a new, dynamic balance? If the reader expects an answer to this question that will give general satisfaction, then he will be disappointed with this book too. Not even theory can provide us with a comprehensive, foolproof answer, let alone documentation, which has to be oriented to the practicable. The Strategy Document published by the United Nations in October 1970 after two years of intensive preliminary work points in the right direction, but a strategy cannot tell us who will ultimately come off best, the strategists or those elements of fate that oppose them as described in the first chapter of this book. There are no ready-made solutions but there are well thought out concepts, and that is more than there was a few years ago. What is their starting-point? It is at first a negative one in that they attach less importance to economic growth. Economic growth is necessary but more as a by-product and a rough indicator than as a target. (It is only logical that we cannot expect the developing countries to reach this conclusion unless we in the industrial countries—on seemingly different grounds—come to a similar conclusion). Then positively in that such concepts plainly establish that there is no alternative but to start from the basic needs of the people.

In this connection I agree with Ivan Illich, though I fail to follow some of his conclusions. "The only possible answer", he says, "to the constantly increasing under-development of the Third World is to meet the basic requirements existing there rather than those that are imported from the developing countries".[17] Certainly, it does not lie in the hands of the German Government to decide which needs are imported into the countries of the Third World; certainly, needs will differ from country to country, and certainly it is not our business to define the needs of others, but the discussion of strategy for the second development decade has shown that it is quite possible to reach agreement on some fundamental requirements. Paragraph 3 of the United Nations

Strategy Document reads: "These people are often undernourished, uneducated, unemployed . . ."

These are the three fundamental requirements that constantly recur—in the plans of the World Bank, in the four or five-year plans of many countries, and also in the policy concept drawn up by the German Government on 11 February 1971 : employment, food, education. The fact that people in the Third World also have many material and non-material needs is obvious : to live in reasonably human conditions—and this is not simply a question of having individual accommodation—to have a chance to preserve or restore their health, social integration, and a distribution of income which does not make a mockery of all concepts of justice.

In this case, too, it is not a question of assimilation; proper nourishment in the Congo need not be the same as in Europe. (Serving deep-frozen chickens from Germany in Kuwait's Hilton Hotel may be in the interests of German agriculture but hardly of Arab cuisine). Education in the Third World can certainly not—perhaps one should say cannot any longer—be an imitation of educational establishments and curricula of 19th century Europe, especially as we ourselves have come to doubt their value. For the great majority of people in the developing countries employment will not for a long time to come mean working in a job requiring investment in the region of $14,000—28,000 (200 million jobs at $14,000 each would cost the astronomical amount of $2,800,000 million). If only for reasons of climate, living accommodation in the Southern hemisphere will be less expensive than in Sweden or Canada. Health care will not mean that every citizen will have a first-class surgeon or a hospital with the most up-to-date medical equipment.

In all these things each country will have to find its own way, and certainly it cannot simply be our way. We are not called upon to export our way of life, our production methods, or our political and social structures, but to help others find their own. The fact that this view only really started to establish itself during the first Decade is certainly one of the reasons why we are faced with such crushing problems in the second.

5. TARGETS FOR THE DECADE

One requires but little imagination to predict that if the second decade continues as it began the alternatives we shall be faced with at the beginning of the third will probably be even more dramatic than they are now. The first year in the second decade did not become a year of special effort on the part of the industrial countries—with the exception of a few, such as the Scandinavian countries. It has thrown important developing countries such as Pakistan and Ceylon further back, and with regard to tariff preferences it brought visible, though by no means spectacular, progress. On the whole it was characterised less by rapid economic progress than by impatience and violence. It cannot be denied that in some important countries the second development decade will prove to be not so much one of rapid growth as one of disappointment, bitterness, unrest and violence, and it is quite im-impossible to tell whether such violence will lead to change, incrustation, or simply the dissolution of political and social structures.

It would therefore seem advisable to set a precise and seemingly modest short-term target for the second decade. If it proves possible in the '70s to improve education, employment, the food and housing situation, health services and social security to such an extent that there will be good prospects of tangible progress with family planning programmes in the '80s, then the second decade will have been a success. Then the decisive link in the chain of misery will have been broken. In pursuing this aim it will not be a question of imposing family planning on anybody but of enabling as many families as possible to decide for themselves the number of children they want. Only then will the third decade have its chance.

This is not to say that family planning should take the place of development aid or indeed become its purpose, but in many countries it is essential if a process is to be started which deserves to be called "development". Just as there is a disastrous connection between the birth rate and want, so too must there be a connection between family planning and the alleviation of want. There is not enough time to wait until a very slow increase in the general level of prosperity, constantly disrupted by political chaos, reduces the birth rate; family planning must therefore become possible and effective before Pakistan or Indonesia can reach the standard of living which Germany enjoyed in the '20s. This will require for the time being not so much the pill or other contraceptives but the mobilisation of the people by means of education and employment, a minimum of social infrastructure and security. Those who are concerned with satisfying fundamental human needs should first concentrate on that which will free people from the compulsion to allow more and more children to grow up into an increasingly less happy future.

But even this seemingly modest target calls for greater efforts than those envisaged in the budgets of the most important developing countries and in the financial plans of the large industrial nations. Pearson's target of 0.7 per cent of the gross national product in the form of official aid was the minimum. If the leading industrial countries continue to find it an unattainable maximum we shall see ourselves in a position, even before we enter the third decade, of having to pay several times more in one form or another. Budget estimates are not the only consideration, however. Concern for the Third World must become a major factor in our overall policy, in our cultural policy (how much attention do our schools give to the Third World?), of our trade policy (how far should we go in reducing the tariffs on goods from developing countries), structural policy (what happens to the textile workers who have to change their job?), science policy (how can suitable technologies be found for the Third World?), agricultural policy (how long can the EEC afford to keep on subsidising 1 million tons of its dear sugar beet every year to lower the price to the world market level so that it can compete with sugar cane from the developing countries?), transport policy (how can transport systems be developed which hold out hope of preventing the rapidly growing conurbations in the developing countries from becoming choked to a standstill by traffic?), defence policy (what would the erosion of political structures in the Indian sub-continent mean in terms of the military balance in Asia and beyond?). And as to environmental protection measures, we have seen already that they can no longer be planned without regard for the Third World.

All this will change the quality of international relations. The only question is whether this change will take place quickly enough. Borrowing an idea from C. F. von Weizsäcker, I once described development policy as a start towards world domestic policy. Some people thought this was a romantic concept, but in fact it is a question of the brutal compulsion of facts which will leave us with no other choice but to seek new ways of settling conflicting interests and new forms of international co-operation.

The Netherlands Minister for Co-operation with the Developing Countries, Mr. B. J. Udink, a man of rather conservative views, said in an address before the Vienna Institute for Development in June 1970 that the great change taking place in our age, the mutation of our whole civilisation, was the integration, the structural fusion of the world into an indivisible economic and social community of interests. In other words, we shall continue to come up against ever more problems which concern the whole world and which can only be tackled on a global basis. Year by year it will be ever more relentlessly brought home to us that the "space-ship Earth" is one entity. This applies not only where the future of the Third World is at stake, but in these countries it will be particularly evident. This will make the world not a more beautiful and simple but a more complicated and dangerous place. It is not a question of creating a wholesome world but of preventing the emergence of a radically unwholesome, non-salutary and possibly incurable one.

III   Points of Departure

1. FAMILY PLANNING

I F THE PRESENT TREND is not broken in the '80s the
human family will be increasing at the rate of about
1,000 million every ten years by the end of this century, whilst at the beginning of the next the same growth
will be achieved in only eight years. It is by no means out
of the question that the children born today will live to
see a world with a population of 15,000 million. And if
the current growth rates are projected still further into
the future we find that the grandchildren of those children will be sharing the earth's surface with 60,000 million
people.

We are told this is improbable, and that is no doubt
true, only the birth rate will not slacken off so quickly
by itself. As we saw earlier on, where employment,
education and the food situation are not improved the
surplus of births does not decrease. And because it does
not the additional millions growing up can hardly be
given a better education or better nourishment, and
only in exceptional cases can they be productively employed. Even in many countries of Africa and Latin
America where there are still thinly populated areas,
overpopulation is not uncommon, for the number of
people who can live on one piece of land depends on the
infrastructure, capital and the available technical
facilities.

There are those in Latin America and Africa who
maintain that family planning is nothing but a clever
invention by the industrial countries to restrict the number and influence of the coloured nations, even to

exterminate them. It is true that family planning is sometimes called for as if it were a panacea that could save us a lot of trouble, and particularly development aid. But in reality family planning can in any case be effective only as one of the means of mobilising the community. In most cases the effect of family planning measures, whether sensible or not, does not begin to tell until the worst of the misery is over. Without better education, food with a higher protein content, more jobs and better medical care, family planning will be fighting a losing battle. And in many cases these programmes cannot be launched at all where antiquated social structures hamper even a frank discussion on the subject. The word is getting around that there can be no solution without family planning; on the other hand, the fact that family planning alone will not solve the problem is obvious. Nobody will be so foolish as to try and impose family planning aid on governments that do not want it, but it may be quite useful to indicate with the aid of demographic studies what the current birth rate implies for a nation's educational system or the employment situation.

The assertion that people in the Third World want a lot of children is only partly true, although it is a fact that in some communities a woman's worth is still determined by the number of sons she brings into the world. Where there is no kind of social security it may be a sensible proposition to have a lot of children because this increases the chances of at least one or two of them surviving and one day earning money with which to tend to the needs of their parents when they are old. All the same, it has been estimated that three million abortions are procured in India every year, and in Latin America the percentage is even higher (indeed in one Latin American country there are said to be three abortions to every birth).

Mothers in the Third World would also prefer to have a few healthy children than a brood of offspring which they cannot adequately care for—that is if they had the choice. The object is not to prevent births at any cost but rather to give families the opportunity to choose the size of family they think they can responsibly manage. In the developing countries the government is the initiator of on average 60 per cent of all family planning measures; in India the percentage is as high as 87. In 1960 three countries had a family planning programme at least on paper. In 1970 there were twenty-five accounting for two-thirds of the total population of developing countries. In other countries the government shuts both eyes if private organisations introduce family planning schemes. Where programmes have been adopted there is often not the organisational network through which the people in need of family planning assistance can be reached. In Ceylon and Taiwan 95 per cent of married couples who want advice can get it, in Pakistan 75 per cent, in Tunisia and Iran 40 per cent, but in Indonesia only 10 per cent.

Where the aim is to reduce the birth rate it is not sufficient to improve and extend existing programmes, to give advisers better training, to increase the number of hospitals and introduce more up-to-date methods of educating the people as to the need for family planning. There are problems to be overcome which have their roots in cultural and religious traditions, or in the rivalries and suspicions among tribes and states. Often there is also a shortage of funds, although ingenious economists have calculated that every birth prevented means a saving of investment in social security, education and employment equivalent to at least two annual incomes. The cost-benefit ratio for family planning is between 1 : 10 and 1 : 30. This seems a crushing disproportion, but it is no more crushing than the situation in Calcutta or Lima.

Some theoreticians go so far as to suggest that a special tax should be levied on families with too many children, a method which surely goes beyond the permissible limits of brutality. In Pakistan parents now forfeit their tax allowance if the government thinks they have too many children. In Singapore state hospitals charge extra for the delivery of fourth and subsequent children. But what may work in Singapore would hardly stand a chance of success in India, simply because it is only in the more progressive countries that children are born in state hospitals. It is not surprising to find that those developing countries that have managed to make a considerable dent in the birth rate are among the more advanced countries of the Third World. In such countries, incidentally, the marriage age is higher, a factor which has contributed at least as much to their success in this field as measures to promote contraception.

On the whole, however, family planning has produced only very moderate results. According to a survey carried out by the OECD, all the family planning programmes together prevented about 2.3 million births in 1968. This means that without family planning the average birth rate in the Third World would have been about 45 instead of 43.8 per thousand. The fact is that up to now no ideal contraceptive has been found that would receive general approval on medical and moral grounds. It would have to be simple, foolproof, without harmful side-effects, and above all cheap. For the time being, therefore, more births will be prevented in the Third World by abortion and sterilisation than by all contraceptives together.

A suitable remedy will not be found so quickly, but it is quite possible that intensive research will discover methods which will reduce the amount of physical and psychological damage. Even today, this would be less than the price that mankind has to pay for boundless population growth. Organisations like the United Nations Fund for Population Activities which are concerned with family planning will be wary of setting ambitious targets. I do not see the slightest chance of reducing the population growth rate to nil by the year

2000, at least not in the developing countries. But if we undertake to try and reduce the growth rate by 1 per cent in the next twenty years, in other words to about 1.5 per cent (in Latin America from about 3.5 to 2.5 per cent a year), this need not be an unrealistic target, not even if the mortality rate continues to decline and the proportion of fertile women increases rapidly. Whether this proves successful will be determined by developments in other spheres, such as education.

2. EDUCATION

People in the developing countries realise that they have to learn. They are regarding themselves more and more as learning communities in which education is the very synonym for human development. Four years ago the President of Tanzania, Julius Nyerere, wrote a report on the subject of Education for Self-reliance. He and many other people, Nyerere said, had time and again called for "more education" for the nation's children, but he doubted whether this was enough. And he goes on:

"It is now time that we looked again at the justification for a poor society like ours spending almost 20 per cent of its Government revenues on providing education for its children and young people, and began to consider what that education should be doing. For in our circumstances it is impossible to devote Shs. 147,330,000/- every year to education for some of our children (while others go without) unless its result has a proportionate relevance to the society we are trying to create."[18]

Similar considerations are today occupying many developing countries. There people are rightly asking whether an educational system developed in an entirely different society and in an entirely different cultural environment is appropriate to their needs, a system

42

which no longer goes unchallenged even in the countries of origin. Nyerere's criticism of his country's school system sounds familiar to us. He maintains, "First, the most central thing about the education we are at present providing is that it is basically an elitist education designed to meet the interests and needs of a very small proportion of those who enter the school system."[19]

The primary schools, he says, aim above all to provide pupils for the secondary school, but 87 per cent never see a secondary school, and the result is that the remaining 13 per cent later go about with a "feeling of superiority" and demand quite a substantial salary as a matter of course. Nyerere therefore recommends an educational system that is oriented to the working world of the great majority of the population, for instance the school farm. The type of education which alienates children from their working environment or indeed causes them to regard that environment with scorn can have devastating consequences. (In a community in which a skilled worker's diploma is something rare and coveted it can very well happen that the holder will acquire a "white collar" complex and feel that from now on he should cease to do the very thing for which he has been trained.)

In the international discussion of education a distinction is made between the "social demand" and the "manpower approach". Social demand means that the educational system should provide the type of training demanded by the population, manpower that it should provide the labour needed in industry and society. The endeavour to meet the social demand has led to a costly expansion of formal school education in the developing countries. Nearly everywhere the principle of general free primary education has become a part of the political programme. In spite of the rapid expansion of the school system the demand for education can be met only to a very limited extent. The school population is increasing but population growth has prevented any appreciable proportionate improvement.

In many developing countries a usually badly adapted educational system which is accessible to only a limited section of the population swallows anything up to one-quarter of the national budget and up to 5 per cent of the gross national product. Where arts subjects predominate and, consequently, science and mathematical subjects are neglected, the contribution of education to the nation's economic progress is small. But worse still is the fact that the curricula, too, are often quite irrelevant to the country's needs.

Education can, and must, help to loosen hardened social concepts and structures to mobilise and dynamise the people, to foster group solidarity, and to create a civic consciousness. Measures in the educational sector cannot be one-sidedly oriented to economic growth; they must be constantly reviewed as to their intended social impact. Educational policy therefore demands not only technocratic expertise but also the courage to assess its political value.

The limited availability of educational opportunities in many developing countries, rather than leading to social integration, aggravates social conflicts. The one who has no opportunity to go to school is worse off than the one who does, even if the latter does not complete the course. There again, the latter possesses neither specialised knowledge nor occupational skills. School leavers who cannot find work lead an insecure existence on the fringe of the cities. The potential inherent in their education is wasted by the frustrations of a heightened conflict between the generations.

We should not deny our own part in all this. Illich is certainly right when he accuses the colonial powers of having left the developing countries with curricula and teaching methods that are oriented to the educational aims of 19th century Europe, the type of school based on theory and discipline. Many of those who attend schools for the elite, which instil neither creative initiative nor equip their pupils with technical skills, are incapable of doing a useful job when they leave. Illich therefore calls for a process of "de-schooling", the abolition of these useless schools which are accessible to only one section of the population and consolidate class distinctions in a most infamous manner. He maintains that compulsory education and the system of qualifications required for admission to careers deceptively suggest that everyone receives the place in society which his performance entitles him to. "For the poor nations compulsory education is a monument of self-imposed inferiority."[20]

According to Illich, the alternative to irrational and expensive general school education is out-of-school education designed to equip young people and adults with the skills they need in everyday life. Here I disagree with him. I do not believe it will be possible to replace the school by the working environment. It is possible, and necessary, to take the working environment to the school and vice-versa. In this respect I find Nyerere's school farms programme more realistic. Nevertheless, Illich's ideas have enriched international discussion on this subject and much of his contribution is reflected in the principle of life-long integrated education advocated by UNESCO. Within this concept education no longer takes place in one institution only and is not confined to a limited phase of the individual's life at the end of which the schooled product is solemnly discharged to enter the life of the community.

"Education is no longer the privilege of an élite or the concomitant of a particular age; to an increasing extent, it is reaching out to embrace the whole of society and the entire life-span of the individual. This means that it must be continuous and omnipresent. It must no longer be thought of as preparation for life, but as a dimension of life, distinguished by continual acquisition of knowledge and ceaseless re-examination of ideas."[21]

For many developing countries life-long education cannot for the time being mean that all children will receive a formal school education. The aim should be to work out alternatives for those who are not reached at all or only inadequately by formal education. This will require the developing countries to work out their own models, for up to now there have been no examples of a mixed system of formal education and different programmes of youth and adult education to go on.

In order to ensure that the many millions who have no opportunity for regular schooling are not left on the periphery, it will be essential to provide non-formal education. In many cases it will thus be possible to reach wider sections of the population than by increasing the school intake. The social environment and the employment situation will have to be analysed to determine whether intensive short courses imparting specific skills, long-term programmes, or on-the-job training will be the more appropriate. This could also include measures to eradicate illiteracy if the conditions for life-long reading exist. Only if what is taught satisfies pupils' actual needs, in other words if education is functional, will its motivating force be strong and hence its success considerable.

In formal school education, too, there must be a relationship between the subject-matter and the realities of daily life. "Functionality", a concept initially postulated for out-of-school primary education, must be applied to all types of education. If it is not functional in terms of society's needs it will miss the mark. This makes changes in curricula and school-leaving qualifications imperative. If efforts to guide the population's educational aspirations in the direction of life-long functional learning prove successful there may open up the prospect of easing the burden on politicians of having to decide between the demand for education and the absorptive ability of the labour market. At present educational aid accounts for about 10 per cent of Third World expenditure in this sphere, so the quantitative contribution of foreign aid to an adequate educational system can only be marginal. But where it is a question of research on methods and forms of organisation which will help to mobilise the people, the industrial countries can provide considerable stimulus. The aim should be to help the developing countries to cope with the legacy we have left them.

3. MOBILISATION OF SELF-HELP

"Thus a group of villages together could organise their servicing station for agricultural implements and farm vehicles; they could perhaps make their own cooking utensils and crockery out of local materials, or they could organise the making of their own clothes on a communal basis. Such villages could also organise together for social, political and educational purposes, so as to bring to all members in their rural area some of the opportunities which can come from living in communities. But all these things would depend upon the democratic decisions of the members themselves.

By such means as these there would be re-established all the advantages of traditional African democracy, social security and human dignity, and at the same time we would have prepared ourselves to take advantage of modern knowledge and the advantages which this can bring."[22]

This is how Julius Nyerere described the Ujamaa village in 1967. It is a fact that people in the developing countries can do a lot with the few means at their disposal. They can sink a well together, build a road or a school; working on a co-operative basis they can buy cheaper and obtain better prices for their crops But this is something new for people to whom disease and want have for centuries been a permanent companion. Many of them still accept their lot as something unalterable or as God's will. They lack the strength and the knowledge with which to tackle the catastrophes, the droughts and the floods which keep on recurring. Undernourished or sick people who have no productive activity will seldom be able to drag themselves out of their lethargy. They need psychological stimulus and material support to enable them to make a start with something unfamiliar and to abandon outdated prejudices.

In regions where progress has hitherto been inconceivable, self-help is a revolutionary concept. It can bring considerable economic improvements, but the mobilisation of people is also an end itself. Where people realise that they can change their situation life for them assumes a new quality, and hope takes the place of resignation. Even in the slum areas of big cities there are not only slums of resignation but also slums of hope. In these areas live people who have summoned up the courage and initiative to leave their familiar surroundings and seek their fortune in the city. Instead they all too frequently find filth, disease and crime. But many of them form self-help organisations, sometimes spontaneously, sometimes with the help of the authorities.

One example is Guatemala City. Of a population of 600,000-plus, 100,000 live in slums—to be more precise, between 200 and 10,000 people are vegetating in each of eighty-seven slum areas and the number increases every year, sometimes by as much as 20 per cent. On the plantations of the big landowners the workers are being replaced by machines. Many of these people now live in canyons on the edge of the city. As if it were not bad enough that there should be no sanitation, the city sewage is channelled to these spots. Electricity is available only in a few places and drinking water is scarce.

There are no police stations, no medical centres, no schools. In theory it is possible for children to attend state schools outside the slum colony, but only half of them do so. Almost one-third of all live-born children die in the first year and another 18 per cent before they reach the age of five. Their parents live from hand to mouth selling lottery tickets or as prostitutes. Regular work is a rarity. Because they have no work they have no money, the children receive no education, and then they too, have no proper work. And that is not the only vicious circle.

It was in these areas that the "aid and advisory service" for the *pobladores*, as the slum inhabitants are called, was born. The idea came not from Guatemala but Chile through discussion with an institute which is in contact with *Misereor*, the Roman Catholic charitable organisation with headquarters in Aachen, Federal Republic of Germany. Nevertheless, all the work is done by the local inhabitants and only occasionally is help given by a few foreigners who are employed elsewhere in Guatemala.

After complete stock had been taken of the situation in 1966, the *Central de Servicios* was founded in 1967 after consultation with *Misereor*. The service has two experts on co-operatives, two assistants, a social worker, a housecraft teacher, and a solicitor with an assistant. Their aim was to show the inhabitants of five colonies how they could help themselves. "Improvement committees" were established which formed themselves into a *Movimiento nacional de pobladores*. And this organisation made sure that the work did not degenerate into a system of paternalistic tutelage by noble-minded helpers.

By 1970 they had run 228 courses, opened 11 co-operative stores, established 49 clubs, installed new water pumps, and constructed sewage systems. The people have begun to live more hygienically and to earn a little more. Is all this a placebo, mere facade? It probably would be if the mentality of the people had not changed

49

as well. They have sensed that what is does not necessarily have to be. The project is likely to peter out one day if in the community as a whole everything stays the same. But can everything stay the same if people realise that the conditions can be changed? Where people are mobilised development takes place.

Another example is the *Cooperación Popular* in Peru. The Belaúnde government had promised to help the villagers in the highlands by providing cheap loans and trained technicians to the same extent that they could help themselves. In 1967 the German Federal Government sent eighteen specialists, most of them engineers, with a few simple vehicles and building machinery to work with the Indios in various parts of the Andes. Since then, the Indios, supervised by the Alcaldes, have built 19 water supply systems for 19,400 people, 31 ordinary roads of a total length of 220 miles, 97 simple irrigation channels for 35,840 acres of land, using picks, shovels and wheelbarrows, and working according to the plans prepared by the experts. More roads and channels are already under construction or in the planning stage.

No one can say exactly how many schools have been built in the meantime, but today hardly any community in the Peruvian highlands is without a school and a medical station. And although they cannot all be used at the moment this is because the government in Lima cannot provide enough teachers and medical staff. After the military coup in 1968, the name of this self-help organisation changed, but not its purpose. When I visited Peru in 1969 the government asked for agricultural advisers. Meanwhile eight German farming experts have gone to Peru to help the highland farmers in their efforts to increase production. They will need to be unassuming in their approach because people who have learnt how to help themselves have acquired a self-confidence which will tolerate advisers only if they are content to be that and nothing more.

4. TECHNOLOGY

The technology applied in developing countries is inadequate for two reasons : neither the methods of production nor what is produced serves the fundamental needs of the people. During the past two centuries, the industrial countries have gradually changed over from labour-intensive to capital-intensive production methods. The machine has relieved man of an increasing amount of work, including many unpleasant, heavy menial tasks. At the same time it has increased productivity. Technology as applied in the industrial countries starts from the assumption that the productive factor "labour" is scarcer than the productive factor "capital". This is the technology the developing countries are faced with today, except that in their case the position is reversed : the productive factor "capital" is scarce whereas the productive factor "labour" is available in abundance.

Even Hitler's autobahns were built with spades and wheelbarrows. Today, the developing countries incur heavy debts to buy modern construction machinery with which to build roads for imported cars. Heavy capital expenditure per worker presupposes considerable wealth. This the developing countries do not have; indeed, such methods tend to have the opposite effect for under these circumstances the jobless millions can never be found productive employment. Even a reduction in the birth rate would only slightly improve the unemployment situation within the foreseeable future since the people who will be looking for work in 1985 have already been born. If a remedy is to be found the developing countries will have to acquire entirely new methods of production and economic planning. Mahatma Gandhi had already realised that it was not mass production but production by the masses that could bring his country progress. This is easier said than done. Many realise that our technology cannot simply be transferred, but what kind of technology should the developing countries have?

The Pearson Report speaks of "frontier technology" and the ILO of "appropriate technology". E. F. Schumacher's term "intermediate technology" is also frequently used. Schumacher heads a working group under this name in London. He also speaks of "self-help technology", by which he means methods of manufacturing simple and cheap goods that are vital to life. There is no doubt that people in both rural and urban districts can resort to self-help and manufacture goods for their own needs, but elements of self-help should also be introduced into mass production processes. Handicraft done in the home may sometimes be preferable to a modern factory.

The ideas which Schumacher put down in writing as early as September 1964 ought surely to have been given more attention.[23] He makes a distinction between a "£100 technology" which is more appropriate to the requirements of the developing countries and the "£1,000 technology" which is customary in industrial countries. He starts from the assumption that in the industrial countries capital costs per job are roughly equivalent to the average annual income of one worker, about £1,000. This means that one job can be created in one man-year, in other words one man would have to save one month's income a year for twelve years to be able to make himself independent. But if one job, as in the developing countries, costs ten times as much as one worker earns, then one man would have to save for 120 years to create one new job. From this Schumacher concludes that countries which pay low wages just cannot afford a £1,000 technology but rather need a £100 version. In his opinion about £70 per job is the most that can be invested in many countries.

Those who advocate "appropriate technology" are often accused of economic irrationality. Certainly, it will seldom be able to compete in world markets with a costly labour-intensive procedure. For exports it is essential to find production methods which with the same or

52

less cost will absorb more labour than hitherto. In India there is an enterprise which applies "£100 production methods". The owner himself has invented semi-mechanical methods of manufacturing stainless steel watch cases and metal wristlet watch straps. He employs a far bigger labour force than would be required to manufacture the same products in Switzerland, but owing to the low capital cost involved he can still compete in world markets and exports his products to all parts of the world, including Switzerland, where he is a subcontractor for the watchmaking industry.

Where production is oriented to the home market or to a regional economic community, higher production costs or inferior quality need not be an obstacle to labour-intensive processes if they reduce the social cost of unemployment. Appropriate tariff barriers are then justifiable if sizeable markets are available in the developing countries.

More serious is the charge of "technological colonialism", the assertion that "appropriate technology" would keep the developing countries on a lower economic level. This theory cannot be refuted, only even if world economic structures changed in favour of the developing countries they would not reach the technological level of the industrial countries for a long time to come. A new universal division of labour with some countries using computers and others sewing-machines can on no account be regarded as satisfactory. But the object is not to achieve the best of all possible worlds but to give hundreds of millions a chance to make a living. It would be technological colonialism if we wanted to continue urging upon the developing countries production methods which leave their surplus labour idle. It is the same with regard to the transfer of our consumer habits. Goods are sold in these countries which were intended for the consumer in an economy geared to the cultivation of demand. Twenty years ago Europeans were not unhappy because they could not buy non-iron shirts in

53

cellophane wrapping. Women in developing countries will not be unhappy because they cannot choose from a full range of cosmetics which very few of them can afford to buy in any case. Expensive packing materials, a planned-for degree of wear and tear which maintains consumption, are harmful luxuries in developing countries.

When Illich says that the road to poverty is paved with technical assistance, he means the introduction of modern consumer goods which a minority at most can afford at the expense of the majority. "The wealthy, those who have received a school education, and the old people of this world try to communicate their dubious blessings by forcing their packaged solutions on to the Third World."[24] It has often been said that drinking Coca-Cola instead of water does not amount to much progress for people in developing countries. It is not without reason that Tanzania, for example, has prohibited the import of luxury goods, including cars above a certain size. If the German press complain about this because, they say, it prevents development of a consumer society,[25] it is an understandable attitude by those who want to export their goods to that country. Yet those who have plans for a balanced process of sociological development must surely do without heart transplants as long as there are many people who cannot even be vaccinated against smallpox.

The kind of innovation which Illich considers to be important is, for instance, the "mechanical mule", an extremely robust vehicle that is cheap to run and will keep going even in the morass during the rainy season and can cope with inaccessible terrain. Speed, comfort and elegance, he maintains, are qualities which the South American peasant would gladly manage without as long as he had a practical means of transport. A German firm appears to be trying to develop a mechanical mule with these practical qualities, but if it is to be cheap and to require little foreign exchange then it will no doubt have to be partly manufactured in the developing countries, even if this were only the assembly stage for a start.

Another firm is at present trying out another machine, a mobile unit no bigger than a motor car which in the coffee and banana growing countries processes the banana stalks which have been cut to produce fibres which can be used for the making of sacks. This will save farmers not only the laborious job of removing the banana stumps but, more important, the cost of importing jute or synthetic sacks for their coffee. In other words, this machine will manufacture from local material what is needed on the spot.

The technological gap one hears so much about cannot be closed simply by exporting our technical achievements. Developing countries must use the appropriate labour-intensive methods to manufacture the goods their people need. In this respect there are still tremendous tasks ahead for applied research, not only in the field of production but also with regard to nutrition and public health. Economic methods of producing protein from algae, a method of eradicating bilharziosis, or simple and safe means of contraception, can be innovations of great significance. Here there are opportunities for research projects designed to establish technologies appropriate to the needs of the developing countries.

5. EMPLOYMENT

It was not until about three years ago that we began to obtain information which at least told us roughly the extent of unemployment and underemployment in the developing countries. According to the ILO World Employment Programme, at least 7.5 per cent of the working population of those countries, that is, about 76 million people, are looking in vain for work.[26] Nobody knows exactly how many people either give up or do not even bother to start the hopeless search for work, how many on the land or in the service industries have only occasional employment or whose work is so unproductive as to be not enough to live on. The estimates of "hidden" unemployment and underemployment vary from country to country between 10 and 50 per cent.[27] On average between 20 and 30 per cent of the labour potential of the developing countries is idle at present. And what is worse, the number of jobs is not increasing as fast as the population of working age because the nature and speed of industrialisation are inadequate to cope with the influx of people from the land in addition to the high population growth in the cities.

By 1980 another 225 million people will be looking for work. For them and for the unemployed of today 300 million new jobs would have to be created by that time.[28] If the present trend continues, however, there will only be an additional 80 million jobs in agriculture and 20 million in industry, so that 200 million would be unemployed.[29] The fact that things have reached this stage has rightly been termed the "most tragic failure of development"[30] of the policy hitherto pursued by developing and industrial countries. Today we must accept that it was naive to expect that enough jobs would be created as a by-product of economic growth and that there is no quick, ready-made solution for the employment problem in developing countries. It will be hard enough at least to prevent the current 20 to 30 per cent of the working population without productive work from increasing to 30 to 40 per cent by 1980. As a first step employment should no longer be regarded as a by-product but as a target of development policy.

Edwin M. Martin, Chairman of the OECD Development Assistance Committee, therefore refers to the employment target in his report as "a central issue for developing countries in drawing up their development plans".[31] No work means no roof over one's head, no education for the children, no share in progress, and no trace of social justice.

The obstacle to this goal is a deep-seated prejudice that employment is achieved at the expense of economic growth. Even the unemployment level in the industrial countries proves this to be wrong,[32] and it is even more wrong in the case of the 20 to 30 per cent of the labour potential in the developing countries who are idle. Certainly, only a small proportion of these people—as, for instance, the growing number of "educated jobless" —have any qualifications, thus any attempts to inject life into the economy after the fashion of the industrial countries are of little help.[32] A whole package of measures are necessary, and these cost money that is missing in other sectors. But where there is such a high level of unemployment the economic advantages are also greater : savings on the social cost of unemployment, better use of scarce capital, and the enlargement of the domestic market. Should a high level of employment—which will be attainable only in exceptional cases for the time being—actually conflict with the aim of economic growth, it will require a political decision as to which is to be valued higher : the basic needs of the hitherto jobless or the opportunities of those who are already better off to increase their income further still.

Since family planning may not bring relief until the late eighties at the earliest (the unemployed of 1985 have already been born) there are three uphill courses available : promotion of the more labour-intensive sectors, more labour-intensive production methods, and immediate employment programmes. On average, 65 per cent of the labour force of developing countries are employed in agriculture,[33] and even in Latin America the proportion is still over 40 per cent.[34] Their contribution to the gross national product is considerably smaller, in many cases not even half as big as their proportion of the labour potential.[35] Although such figures are to be viewed with caution, they nevertheless show that agriculture will have to improve productivity and at the same time, at least in the medium term, remain the biggest source of employment. Even if less than 60 per cent were employed on the land by 1980, the absolute labour force in agriculture would increase by 80 million.[36]

Traditional farming methods require very little capital. Bigger yields per unit of area can be achieved by injecting more capital or more labour. Whereas in the industrial countries the aim is to increase the return per worker by investing more capital, many developing countries will first have to achieve a high yield per acre by increasing labour. Development policy must not only promote agriculture because it produces food, commodities and export goods but must guide the "green revolution" in such a way that as many people as possible can work more productively with the smallest possible amount of capital. This means, for instance, that new varieties and crops which will give a greater yield only through intensive cultivation are more important than labour-saving agricultural machinery.[37]

A labour-intensive and at the same time efficient system of agriculture requires irrigation, roads, advisory, credit and sales organisations for small farms and co-operative societies, simple and robust equipment, storage facilities, but also practical basic education, health services, and the will and ability on the part of the jobless illiterates on the land to help themselves. Only in this way can the mass of small farmers, tenants and labourers in many hundreds of thousands of villages create a basis for their existence and resist the attraction of the cities.

In many countries this presupposes that the land is placed at the disposal of the people who actually cultivate it. Such structural changes must not only be carefully planned and organised, they also cost money and must often be enforced in the face of bitter resistance from the rural gentry and the hitherto privileged urban industries. But as it is hardly possible to stop the flight from the land altogether and the population of the cities will therefore continue to grow faster than the national rate—at present almost twice as fast—investment must also be made in other labour-intensive and productive sectors of the economy.

These include, for instance, the building trade, handicrafts, transport and tourism, but also some branches of industry, such as clothing and shoe manufacturing, processing of agricultural products, branches of the electrical industry, metal-working and engineering, are more than average labour-intensive. Some developing countries can therefore already compete in the markets of industrial countries. They could meet a larger proportion of our requirements if there were no protectionist obstacles to prevent them.

As a result of the policy pursued up to now by the developing and industrial countries it is mostly the capital-intensive branches of industry, companies and methods of production that have been promoted. Low interest rates for investment and relatively high wages for the small group of skilled workers, technicians, managers and foreign experts, favourable exchange rates and loans for the import of machinery—not for the financing of domestic costs—preferential treatment for big prestige projects, the thoughtless transfer of the production methods of the industrial countries by foreign and domestic investors, all this could lead to a situation where an increasingly smaller proportion of the population can, through their work, just about keep the heads of the rest above water.

As a first step developing and industrial countries should cease giving preference to capital-intensive industries. In order to do this they will have to review, adjust and supplement their methods of promotion. It is not true that capital-intensive methods are absolutely necessary in most branches of industry. There are very few industries, oil refineries, for instance, that do not include

59

stages of production in which less capital and more labour could be used. Raw materials can be put in manually, semi- or fully automatically, and most factories can manage without packing and automatic accounting machines. There is no need for self-service stores where any number of shop assistants are available, a crane where tackle will do, or a bulldozer if 100 or 1,000 men can do the same work using pick and shovel. And finally a glance at any catalogue of machinery will show that, apart from automatic systems which are worthwhile only if produced in large numbers, there are more simple, more robust and cheaper machines which are equally profitable in smaller quantities.

Our own phase of reconstruction after the second world war was likewise not primarily achieved with the aid of extensive capital and foreign exchange resources, but by hard work and much improvisation. Labour-saving production methods did not become necessary until we reached the level of full employment. What the developing countries need is capital-saving rationalisation. Their plant must be worked to capacity in several shifts and treated with much greater care than in our country. They can manage without sophisticated technical apparatus and frequent changes from one type to another if the machinery they have only lasts longer and can stand greater strain.

Developing and industrial countries alike must realise that the composition and quality of production should not simply be oriented to our surplus society. The developing countries depend on exports to be able to pay for vital imports and must therefore offer products which meet demand and quality standards in the industrial countries, and this, as a rule, calls for standardised production with modern machinery and specialist personnel. But for the large and hitherto neglected home market capital and consumer goods need not be up to these standards. They must rather satisfy the basic needs of the population. Many of the products required can be manufactured by small indigenous factories requiring little capital. Bicycles and ploughshares are more important than gleaming Cadillacs and fully mechanised threshers. Food, clothing and transport for the broad mass of the population provide more employment than a consumer goods industry catering for the needs of a small upper class.

Even if every effort is made to create more jobs in this way, the unemployment and underemployment situation in the developing countries cannot be completely rectified but at best improved. And we can be sure that not everything will be done. Unemployment will hit young people hardest of all. Some countries must try to find work for at least some of their jobless youths with urban and rural district labour services. Little as this may be to our taste—who can blame them?

6. Industry and Agriculture

When the colonial era came to an end many of the countries concerned felt that their industrialisation had been impeded by the former rulers or permitted only to the extent that it served their interests. Thus, although iron-ore was mined in North Vietnam the smelting was done in France in spite of the fact that the ore had to be transported half way round the world. That was the prevailing idea of a division of labour based on the principle that the colonial territories provided the raw materials whilst the industrial countries kept the manufacturing for themselves. No wonder that these countries nowadays regard industrialisation as a means of overcoming their economic dependence on their former colonial rulers, not merely as an economic process but as an element of political emancipation.

This explains the tremendous efforts of many developing countries to accelerate the process of industrialisation in the first few years after gaining independence. Understandably, they concentrated on products intended to replace imports. As the Pearson Report shows, the developing countries achieved an average rate of industrial growth of seven per cent between 1950 and 1967. This is more than the general growth of GNP, which averaged 5 per cent. This achievement is all the more amazing if we consider the unfavourable conditions that prevailed. There was a shortage of skilled labour, power supply, transport, and in many cases spare parts as well. But the Pearson Report makes no secret of the fact that the substitution of imports cannot be continued indefinitely. Many local industrial products, which are protected by tariff barriers, are more expensive to produce than imported goods of similar quality.

On the other hand, it is difficult for the developing countries to sell manufactures and semi-manufactures in world markets. The industrial and technological lead of the industrial countries can only be reduced where the goods produced by the developing countries are cheaper and more favourably located. Finally, tariff barriers or import quotas prevent these countries from exporting large quantities of goods to industrial countries. The seven per cent growth rate therefore hides the fact that the process of industrialisation has differed quite considerably from country to country. Some Latin American and East Asian countries have experienced considerable success whereas others have made hardly any progress at all. Measures aimed specifically at industrialisation have not had the desired effect because other sectors of the economy have not always grown at the same pace. Where energy supply and communications cannot be improved as necessary, production falters. Where the purchasing power of the mass of the population cannot be increased it is difficult to sell the manufactured products, not to mention the goods intended for foreign markets and therefore subject to international competition.

Especially in countries where huge industrial establishments were built on grounds of prestige, there have been frequent setbacks, with the result that these establishments soon changed into "development ruins" or plant which swallowed more subsidies than they yielded profit. On top of this, industrialisation has placed the developing countries more and more in debt with the industrial countries. So what was originally intended as a means of removing their dependence on the industrial countries has, for the time being at any rate, created a new kind of dependence: the mounting indebtedness of the developing countries.

Are the critics right, those who from the very beginning viewed the industrialisation policies of the Third World with scepticism because they thought that industry could only be developed via the trades and small industries, as was the case in our country? Are those right who maintain that the developing countries should concentrate entirely on agriculture? Most of them have realised that neglect of agriculture has bitter consequences. They are agrarian countries only to the extent that the proportion of industrial production is small, not in the sense that they have a healthy, productive agricultural sector. Nearly everywhere the traditional cultivation methods still prevail, single-crop systems, in many cases coupled with extensive farming. Only in exceptional cases do cultivation techniques reach the standards of industrial countries. Moreover, outdated social structures in many areas are an obstacle to increased productivity.

In Latin America, for instance, land, owing to the feudal system of ownership, is not put to maximum use because the owners have no interest. Large areas lie fallow or are used as pasture, even though maize or corn could be grown there. Many developing countries still have to import food. For them, therefore, the first priority is to provide for themselves. At the same time, agriculture would seem, for the next few years at least, to be a more suitable proposition than industry as a means of absorbing the jobless and underemployed. It does not require such high standards of training and industry, and at the same time the techniques developed by the industrial countries can be applied more speedily and with less friction in this than in other sectors. The use of fertiliser, new seed varieties or irrigation methods does not require more schools but at the most a well-functioning broadcasting service for the rural population and a number of transistor radios. In India, Pakistan and the Philippines, where new seed varieties have been used, harvests have been increased many times within a short period. It would certainly be wrong to conclude that industrialisation in the developing countries should be discontinued for this reason. Agriculture and industry do not exclude each other; it is at most a question of priority.

Take Algeria, for instance, a country which has oil, gas, iron-ore and coal deposits, and a well-developed road system from the colonial era. Obviously, Algeria concentrates her efforts on the petrochemical, steel and processing industries. She hopes to earn foreign exchange from the export of oil and gas, and at the same time to save exchange through her own steel production. It is proposed to channel these financial resources to the development of the whole economy, including agriculture.

Taiwan, by contrast, has hardly any mineral resources worth mentioning. As land reform was urgently necessary, priority was given to agricultural development and to earning foreign exchange from the export of agricultural products, funds which are now to be used to build up the nation's industries. Taiwan has had so much success with this policy that in the past few years it has no longer required development aid from the United States. In fact, it sends its own agricultural experts to Asian and African developing countries.

Here, too, of course, there are no generally binding principles for determining the proportion of investment in agriculture and industry, but there is certainly a connection between industrial and agricultural development. Progress in the field of agricultural production soon reaches a limit unless industry creates the purchasing power for more and better foodstuffs. And where heavily populated industrial centres can only be fed with the aid of scarce foreign exchange, the process of industrialisation is soon blocked. Industrialisation does not necessarily mean the rapid growth of cities. Where such measures are introduced in small rural centres they check the drift from the land.

Migration from the land in developing countries has assumed hitherto unknown proportions in the past ten years. The peripheral districts of the cities are often transformed overnight. Where yesterday there were open fields, hundreds of people have today settled in quickly made clay or corrugated-iron huts. The number of new settlers increases not uncommonly by more than 10 per cent a year. Few inhabitants of the city itself concern themselves about whether the people in the suburbs have drinkable water, what happens to their waste, and whether their dilapidated huts will withstand the next big storm or the rainy season.

Yet if life under these conditions is found preferable to an existence on the land, obviously it is because the city in most developing countries offers the best chance of survival. Although the fast growing districts on the outskirts appear to be suffocating the rest of the city, the city does manage to feed its inhabitants somehow. Many people may only live on the left-overs of the upper class but it is enough for an existence from hand to mouth. Often this is more than what is available on the land after a poor harvest. And many of them live in hope of one day being able to clear the hurdle that lies between the seamy quarters of the suburbs and the city centre with its bright lights, multi-storeyed houses and busy streets. And perhaps they also hope to be able one day to buy the things displayed in the windows of the big shops. Where the gap between town and country can be measured not merely in centuries but sometimes in millenia it is not surprising that even life in the slums may seem attractive. If one of them manages to find regular work and then an assured livelihood in the city proper, the news spreads quickly through the shanty areas and penetrates even to the most remote districts. And then others set out to try their luck and thereby reduce the chances of those who have been waiting for years.

When will this flow of people from the country into the cities stop, or at least decrease? Even attempts by force to prevent these people from settling on the fringe of the cities have failed. Probably this migration in the developing countries will continue as long as the land has still less to offer than the city slums. Here, too, nothing adjusts itself alone.

Whereas the upswing in the industrial countries occurred—as Baade proves—simultaneously with the migration of labour from the land into the cities, the decision as far as the developing countries are concerned will be taken on the land, at least in the years immediately ahead. In those countries agricultural production must be boosted to such an extent that people at least do not have to go hungry. Infrastructure must be improved, schools, medical stations and roads built, and above all jobs provided. Otherwise there is no hope for urbanisation either. Cities can die, as the industrial countries have of late come to realise.

7. SOCIAL CHANGE

Development policy must induce the majority of people to consider their situation and make them capable of changing it. But as soon as it does this it meets with resistance, with traditional habits, outdated privileges, antiquated institutions, and powerful group interests. Every doctor, teacher, agricultural expert, every en-

66

gineer, government adviser and volunteer has experienced that. Whether the purpose is to set up a health service in the country, to distribute the waters of a reservoir, or to determine the location of an industry, time and again they come up against walls and barriers. If a few big landowners have the best land, control trade in seed, fertiliser and equipment, if they buy up the harvests and determine who shall have access to credit, water, justice or the government, then an irrigation channel, a development bank, a pilot farm or an agricultural extension service will be of little help to the small farmers and tenants. If the educational system serves to confirm the right of a small minority to an easy job, then those who have attended technical schools will also want to take up a white collar job. If the importers in the ports control the economy then it will be a long time before new inland infrastructures lead to industrialisation. If the trade unions are content to negotiate for a few thousand industrial workers in the cities wages which are unattainable for the mass of their countrymen, then there is little point in the trade unions of the industrial countries supporting them.

If, as in Latin America, five per cent of the population command about 31 per cent of the national income while 40 per cent of the people have to manage on nine per cent,[38] if the consumption of luxury goods, speculation and the flight of capital soak up a large proportion of savings, then it will be a long time before private enterprise and mass consumption bring general prosperity. It is the very experience of practical development policy which shows how necessary reforms are in agriculture, education, taxation, administration, and regional policy. And all too large a proportion of development aid is lost because it is not linked with such reforms.

Social reforms in the Third World are in many cases the critical test for systems which cannot even cope with ordinary day-to-day tasks efficiently. Some point to the lack of suitable foundations and funds as the excuse for postponing reforms. Others say it is sufficient to remove a privileged group or institution and the rest will come of its own accord. Certain as it is that social change in the Third World is inevitable, and equally certain as it is that in some cases edifices of power will have to be broken down, I am less than ever convinced by that naive faith in the "Revolution" which manifests itself from time to time. As if the birth rate would then immediately decrease and production increase, corruption vanish and the administration function! And for most countries of the Third World the matter is too serious for the situation to be cured by tackling one aspect only. The drift from the land and urbanisation are causing socialist Tanzania the same problems as liberal, capitalist Ivory Coast. We know that revolution and shoddiness do not exclude each other, and not only from the speeches of Fidel Castro. The fact that such a country, in spite of its considerable success in mobilising the people and fighting illiteracy, can also be ruined by the chopping and changing of a great leader who every few years proclaims a different economic policy is surely better known to Castro than to his admirers. Where radical social change becomes inevitable they give a nation no more than the chance to make a fresh but laborious start under its own steam. And the argument for this will not be that everything is better afterwards but that things could no longer continue as they were. Hence those countries where progress does continue, step by step, from reform to reform, even though there may not be many of them, are to be envied.

8. FOREIGN TRADE

In the majority of developing countries the most up-to-date sectors of agriculture and industry are geared to export trade. They provide the industrial countries with

68

cheap primary products : food, drink and tobacco, vegetable and mineral raw materials. On the other hand, most manufactured goods, especially capital goods required for industrialisation, have to be imported. This legacy of the colonial era we call "the world-wide division of labour".

West Europeans, Japanese and North Americans owe their prosperity more or less to trade. Trade grows at a faster rate than the gross national product. The share of the developing countries in this source of prosperity has steadily shrunk over the past twenty years. In 1950 they accounted for almost 32 per cent of the world's exports, but in 1969 only 17.7 per cent.[39] True, the export earnings of the developing countries increased by almost 150 per cent during this period, but that of the industrial countries by over 420 per cent.[40] Why? Because demand for manufactures increases faster than demand for primary products, and because the prices of manufactured goods have increased in comparison with the prices of raw materials.

The figures are unmistakably clear : exports of industrial countries have increased fourfold since 1950 and earnings more than five times, whereas the developing countries were able to increase their export earnings only at the same rate as their volume of exports, that is, two and a half times;[41] their terms of trade have deteriorated by about seven per cent since 1950.[42]

That would not be so bad if the commodity element of world trade had not dwindled at an even faster rate —from 44 per cent in 1960 to 33 per cent in 1969— than the proportion of basic commodities to the exports of developing countries—from 85 per cent in 1960 to 76 per cent in 1969.[43]

Up to 60 per cent of the exports of three quarters of all developing countries consists of three raw materials, and 50 per cent of the earnings of half of them comes from one single basic commodity.[44] So for the time being, most developing countries will have to earn the greater part of the foreign exchange they need for development purposes in international commodity markets. From the industrial countries they demand better and more stable commodity prices and the abandonment of any measure that constitutes an additional impediment to their slow growth of imports. Comparable demands by agriculture, mining and stagnant branches of industry in developed countries are seldom so urgent but frequently more successful. These sectors usually receive help to improve productivity and sales and receive cost-reducing subsidies. If this, too, is of no avail, labour and capital can be employed more productively in other spheres.

The market situation differs from one commodity to another but the developing countries rarely find themselves in a strong position. They come up against the protected products of the industrial countries, such as cereals, meat, dairy products, sugar, vegetable oil and fats—and they have to compete against direct or indirect substitutes, as in the case of coffee, tea and cocoa, but above all rubber, jute and fibres, or they are dependent on fluctuations of demand and the buying policies of industrial countries. This applies to metals, ores and mineral oil.

Producers seldom co-operate even though this is their only chance of exploiting their market opportunities, say, in the case of ores and oil, and of avoiding over-production which sometimes occurs with tea and coffee. The course of the 1971 oil negotiations shows that the industrial countries can pay substantially higher prices : a 20 per cent increase in the commodity price works out at only a penny or two per gallon. Every commodity market has its pitfalls and not every concession is of long-term benefit to the developing countries as this could increase their dependence on single commodities. But how long the lean stretch will last before industrialisation is achieved also depends on their commodity earnings. Developing countries must themselves make greater efforts to produce cheaper goods on a tight schedule, but they cannot simply be palmed off with a reference to a market situation which is for the most part determined by the industrial countries who are oriented to a market economy system. The Western industrial countries, being the buyers, not only call the tune in world commodity markets but also export more commodities than the developing countries, 49.5 per cent compared with 40 per cent.[45]

Commodity agreements are not the complete answer, of course, but they can help to place the export earnings of developing countries on a more stable basis. Buffer stocks and supplementary financing will not only keep consumers constantly supplied but will help to stabilise the earnings of developing countries. A particularly sensible solution is to supplement commodity agreements by measures for the diversification of exports. The Federal Republic of Germany is therefore participating in the first experiment of this kind. It is making a contribution of DM 11 million to the Diversification Fund of the International Coffee Agreement.

However important commodity exports may be for the industrialisation of the developing countries, the "markets of tomorrow" will be those for manufactures and semi-manufactures. Between 1950 and 1968 exports of goods in these categories increased at an above average rate : in the industrial countries five times, in the developing countries 3.5 times,[46] which is a fair achievement. In the sixties the developing countries were even able to increase their share of the world market from 5.5 to 6.5 per cent.[47] The greater proportion of these exports come from about a dozen semi-industrialised developing countries and they are often intended for other developing countries. Twelve developing countries account for about three quarters of the exports of manufactures and semi-manufactures. Manufactures make up about one quarter of trade among developing countries —which is very limited, incidentally—but only just under one seventh of their trade to industrial countries.[48]

Manufactures are obviously the answer to the problem of expanding trade between the developing countries, which is growing slowly and consists primarily of trade in food and oil. The markets of industrial countries, which have more purchasing power, would be more interesting of course, but this is the very field where the outsiders lack experience and where the trade barriers of the industrial countries are particularly discouraging. Whereas commodities can often be exported duty-free to industrial countries, the tariff rises sharply at each level of processing. If 60 per cent of manufacturing costs are accounted for by commodities then even a moderate 20 per cent tariff for the manufactured product would afford effective protection for the processing of commodities in the industrial countries, which have imported them duty-free.[49] In addition, about 30 per cent of the manufactures and semi-manufactures from developing countries are subject to quantitative restrictions, and these goods account for three quarters of the imports from those countries, including textiles, clothing and processed agricultural products.[50]

On 1 July 1971, the tariff preferences accorded to the developing countries by the European Economic Community came into force. Tariff preferences for the developing countries had first been called for in 1958. They did not materialise at the first United Nations Conference on Trade and Development in 1964, but were adopted at the second held in New Delhi in 1968. The terms of the basic decision sound revolutionary. All industrial manufactures and semi-manufactures may now, without exception, enter the Common Market entirely duty-free—and one might be inclined to forget that in the case of 150 agricultural products the tariffs have merely been lowered to a varying degree. But there are enough built-in checks with regard to manufactures and semi-manufactures also. Only certain quantities will be duty-free, the total amount being approximately one thousand million dollars but nevertheless it is about twice as much as the amount imported in 1968. The European Community has been particularly cautious with regard to the so called "sensitive" products, about 60 per cent of total imports from developing countries. This applies in particular to textiles and shoes. Common Market members have very nicely distributed the burden among themselves (Federal Republic of Germany 37.5 per cent, France 27.1 per cent, etc.), which does not exactly suggest a common approach, and any imports over and above the quotas are subject to duty as before, so there can be no question of a revolutionary step, but a start has been made.

In any case, more generous concessions on the part of the European Community would probably not have benefited the developing countries at the moment, for only a few of their exporters have goods to offer which the European market can absorb, and fewer still are the exporters with enough experience to spot the gaps which open up in the Community. Now the important thing is to exploit the preferences which are the result of such arduous negotiations, for although the developing countries have in recent years managed to replace imported goods with their own products, the "trade gap" is increasing. Up to now it has been plugged by loans, with commercial credits accounting for only one quarter of outstanding debts but, on account of the hard terms, for half of the debt servicing.

In 1969 the official or officially guaranteed debts of the developing countries were in the region of 60,000 million dollars and the annual debt servicing of eighty-one developing countries had reached the figure of 5,300 million dollars. It increases at the rate of about 15 per cent a year—twice as fast as export earnings, and more and more countries see their debt servicing nearing the critical figure of 20 per cent of their export earnings. Unless there is a change of policy even increased development aid will evaporate in this way. The loss of every further per cent of world trade is for the developing countries equivalent to 20 per cent of the total transfer of capital from Western industrial countries.[51]

9. The Role of Development Aid

From family planning to foreign trade, from education to social change, the developing countries are for the most part dependent upon themselves. That has already been the case up to now. On the average only 10 per cent of investments and 20 per cent of the imports of developing countries have been financed from development aid, in other words from grants or from "soft" loans.[52] The rest has to be earned by exporting goods and services and, where commercial credits are concerned, repaid with interest in hard currency to exporters and investors in industrial countries. What determines the success or failure of the developing countries, therefore, is the amount they can raise themselves and how they use it. Average saving of 15 per cent means for the developing countries a more impressive cut in consumption than 21 per cent of the per capita income in developing countries, which is ten times greater. By 1980 the developing countries hope to be saving as much as 20 per cent of their income.[53]

To the industrial countries 0.35 per cent of GNP for development aid is no more a tangible sacrifice than 0.7 per cent, double the amount. After all, what is $714.3 million* or $1,428.6 million* when the gross national product of the Federal Republic of Germany is $194,286 million and investments worth $51,428* million? But double the amount of aid could increase developing countries' investments by 10 per cent or their national income by about 1.5 per cent. This could make all the difference between stagnation and progress;

* Figures 1971 based on $1 = DM 3.50.

74

it could see them through the worst period until population growth can be substantially retarded. Development aid will bring such success only if it helps the developing countries achieve progress through their own efforts, and that means where the decisions are taken. What counts is the quality of the instruments and where they are applied.

Today, such important developing countries as India, Pakistan and Indonesia are dependent on foreign exchange through development aid for 30 to 35 per cent of their income,[54] and it is to be expected that the growing debt burden will place other countries in a similar position. Even in the case of smaller countries, which, incidentally, receive a relatively large proportion of the development aid made available, the industrial countries cannot shirk their responsibility on the ground that their aid is only marginal. The results achieved in the sectors of agriculture, transport and energy, for instance, show that development aid generates powerful impulses which can determine the speed and direction of progress, even though the figures may not be very impressive.

All too often, however, development aid has been used to promote programmes that have bypassed the basic needs of the people. In some cases, for instance in the field of education, the exclusion of labour-intensive production methods, or credit-tying, its influence has even caused the meagre funds of the developing countries to be misdirected. Some right-wing cynics see this as a confirmation of their prejudices against the developing countries, whilst there are those on the left who would rather dispense with development aid altogether. Both overlook the fact that the industrial countries—partly, but not solely, as a result of development aid—are helping to decide the future of the developing countries whether they want to or not. Development aid must be coupled with the efforts of the developing countries themselves; they can now either fail together or succeed together.

IV Instruments

1. BEGINNING AND TEETHING TROUBLES OF OUR DEVELOPMENT AID

GERMANY'S INITIAL development aid measures ensued neither from an internal revolution nor from a refined aid strategy but from outside impulses and a large element of chance. When President Truman announced his four-point programme in 1949, the obvious thing was for the nations of Europe, who had been helped to their feet by the Marshall Plan, to relieve the United States of part of this new burden. I still remember the warning given by President Kennedy in the summer of 1962 during a talk with members of Henry Kissinger's international seminar, of which I was one, that several European countries tended to shy away from this joint task. It was above all the Germans, who had meanwhile become prosperous again, who were meant.

The Germans were by no means merely unhappy about this. In fact some of them felt it was a moral relief to be able at last to participate in an undertaking which quite obviously was one of the more purposeful and respected in modern times. They were glad to be able to help after having been helped themselves. More important no doubt was the opportunity this gave the Federal Republic of Germany to return to the scene of international politics, for after all development aid could also come in useful in countries that were considering recognising East Germany, the DDR. Moreover, the export trade would benefit too. The developing countries became the "markets of tomorrow", though no one added that they could only become our market to the extent that we were prepared to become theirs.

Nobody could expect that mature projects would be immediately available. Even now, after a period of fifteen years, there is still much to be learnt in the field of development aid, so how would it have been possible to have a specific plan at hand right from the start? True, the aid-upon-request procedure was applied, in other words possible projects were assessed until the developing countries concerned submitted a specific request, but in the early sixties the authorities in some developing countries found difficulty in preparing and presenting such a request in a suitable form, so that some governments were unhappy when German firms or business interests came forward to help, for, after all, these people knew which projects had the best chance of being accepted by ministerial departments. If applications were accompanied by profitability calculations or order lists, so much the better. In many cases a government official's preference for one particular country or sector also left its mark. Technical assistance projects were sometimes sought for one or several experts who had offered their services. Correspondence between a former scholarship holder and the German professor who prepared him for his doctorate led to a university partnership in the form of a project which came to Bonn as a government application, all done in the proper fashion.

The embassies, who had been expected to provide initial reports, were likewise overstrained. Naturally, an ambassador will be inclined to do the government of the host country a favour, for after all it is his duty to foster good relations. And if this provides a little publicity at dedication ceremonies and during visits to the projects, so much the better. In view of all this, it is surprising that so many sensible projects did actually materialise. A technical school whose former pupils find suitable jobs is never a wrong investment whatever the motives behind its origin. And the few pilot farms which caused discouraged local farmers to stand and gape in amazement, but of course not to imitate, soon had to give way to co-operative schemes or extension projects. The tendency to establish large-scale spectacular steelworks soon declined when it was seen that the risk was too great. And the brilliant idea of setting up factories in Africa using obsolete German textile machinery did the taxpayer more harm than it did some German companies good, so that this policy too was quickly abandoned. (One recipient country had to reduce the prices of its own cotton goods drastically, otherwise they would have been far too expensive—the veteran machinery cost too much to maintain.) Then there was the time when an African head of state on an official visit to Germany was so delighted with Bonn's "white mice", that is, the white uniformed motor cyclists who escort foreign leaders through the city, that he put in a request for some and got them. But this kind of aid was short-lived, especially as the motor cycles, having been granted on political grounds, were after all used to escort a visiting minister from East Germany. Nor are there likely to be any more examples of would-be electricians being trained in an engineering department built with German assistance and shown how to handle German-type plugs and sockets which were used nowhere else in that country outside the university.

This was certainly not the only occasion where our own standards and systems were transferred to developing countries too much as a matter of course. In the field of educational aid in particular, it took some time to realise that our own system, which not everybody in our country is still convinced is all that good for us, might be even less suited to the needs of others. And it took us a decade to grasp that preoccupation with economic growth figures can ultimately jeopardise economic growth. Many people learnt from the example of Pakistan that economic growth, if it is not accompanied by social progress, will be negated by social and political crises. In spite of all the improvements, the fact that good projects also failed to have any considerable effect unless they were incorporated in an overall plan continued to be a cause of dissatisfaction. Roads which were seldom used by lorries because the proposed factories had not been built, technical schools whose former pupils could not find suitable work, agricultural projects whose surplus production could not be sold or could not be taken to market for lack of transport are examples of this.

Yet the low proportion of success during the first development decade cannot merely be imputed to irrational decisions by the industrial countries. National prestige and inadequate administration in the developing countries have also been to blame. Although governments have made modern laws they have been neither willing nor able to implement them and therefore not always made the best use of development aid. Where there has been a spirit of social reform there has not been the administrative capacity to turn it into practical policy.[55] Thus it has proved necessary—both nationally and internationally—to create a plan, a strategy, which would guarantee the more effective employment of available funds.

2. TECHNICAL AND EDUCATIONAL ASSISTANCE

Technical assistance is not by any means always synonymous with technology in the strict sense of the word. It is the international term for all forms of personnel aid, whether it takes the form of an apprentice workshop, the search for groundwater, advice for a development bank or the training of nurses, the preparation of urban traffic plans or an extension service for small farmers. The figures for technical assistance are not overwhelming but its share of official aid is increasing rapidly. In 1968 technical assistance commitments were valued at $68,625,000 whilst in 1971 the figure was $135,500,000.

If development aid is to help other nations to find their own way, their own types of production and organisation, then the technical assistance expert is not required simply to transfer his knowledge but to work together with the people in developing countries and use his knowledge in the search for working methods which are appropriate to the country's needs. Only a few of the 785 government-sponsored technical assistance projects currently in progress were wrongly planned from the start. Where a project is not working properly there is usually a lack of co-operation with the authorities of the host country, or the project manager is overburdened when he has to have the nerve and patience to surmount ever new—to him incomprehensible—obstacles and at the same time be firm and friendly towards his German and local colleagues, otherwise a project can breed quarrels and resentment. Considering this, I am not surprised that the one or the other project comes to grief; indeed I am amazed how many experts manage to cope with these tasks. It is now generally appreciated that the training of experts calls for more than languages and know-how. Where an expert fails it is rarely because he does not understand his work but because others do not understand him and he them.

We have seen that in the case of most developing countries the decision in the years ahead will lie on the land. Only if the people on the land can be kept there will the cities gain the breathing space they need for their development. This is the purpose of the Tarquist technical assistance project in Morocco which I visited in May 1971. The aim of the project is "the modernisation of agriculture and forestry in a rural district of the Central Rif range". In the early sixties FAO experts had worked out a general plan for an area of 7,200 square miles in the Western Rif range, one of the poorest regions of Morocco. There the population density is twice, *per capita* income hardly half, the national average. The more the population increased (3.4 per cent a year) the higher up the mountainside the farmers tried to work the land, the steeper therefore the incline, and the more merciless the erosion.

The pitiful amount of wheat still produced on these washed-out slopes is barely enough to provide seed for the next spring. And as the people and the goats have destroyed the woodland on top the water cuts ever deeper furrows in the red clay every year. Anybody who flies over the mouth of the Nekor river can see from the red blotch half a mile wide in the blue waters of the Mediterranean what happens to the fertile soil of the Rif farmers. Every year 2 per cent of the cultivated land is lost in this way, half of it in twenty-five years. It is a vicious circle : the more the farmers look for fresh land the less they have in an area where two-thirds of all the land has a gradient of over 25 per cent. Where the water can no longer be held back the floods also destroy the lowlands downstream.

This is where the German project came in. After the area had been selected—first 1,360 acres and a further 2,000 acres since 1971—the German experts started to fight erosion. Under their direction an area of eighty acres right on top was afforested and every farmer was offered a sheep for every goat, which was a good bargain for all concerned. Low Roman-style stone walls were built in the ravines to hold the water and reduce its flow. River beds were regulated. The recipe is simple : on top the forest, in the middle tree planting, especially almonds (51,000 of them have meanwhile been planted), and in the valleys intensive farming. The farmers on the Rif range see that their harvests can be improved by synthetic fertilisers, but there is also a credit scheme to enable them to buy the fertilisers. They learn about new seed and how to use it, their sheep, cattle and rabbit breeds are improving in quality, and they learn that by growing fodder more of these animals can be fed. The government proposed to apply the results of this experiment to a whole province as from 1972. Of course, the project is open to criticism. If it were only a matter of improving the rate of economic growth then the $2 million or so which will have been spent on it between 1968 and 1973 could have been put to better use elsewhere. Even though farmers can increase their income this makes little difference in terms of the economy as a whole, but it is a different matter where the cost of labour is concerned. Whereas an industrial job in the city costs about 20,000 dirham only 2,500 dirham are required to secure and improve the existence of a farming family. True, one day the question will again arise where the surplus children will find work. Perhaps by then jobs in industry will be available, but for the present the alternative to farming in the hills is unemployment in the towns.

Educational aid accounts for an increasing proportion of personnel aid. Today it already ranges from the reorganisation of primary schools to learning by television and university partnerships, and from the technical school to radio for farmers and adult education. In many cases it is the seemingly small, and therefore cheap, projects which prove to be the more successful. In March 1970, for instance, Erich Avemann, a teacher, began as an adviser to the Peruvian ministry of education, not in Lima but 10,500 ft high up in the Andes 560 miles away. He had worked for eight years at the *Colegio Alexander von Humboldt* in Lima. During this period he wrote reading and arithmetic books for primary schools, lectured to Peruvian students on teaching methods, and helped at the University of San Marcos to train teachers from mountain villages where the people spoke only Quechua.

Now Avemann is revising the teaching methods in these villages. His aim is to teach the Quechua-speaking Indio children to speak Spanish in such a way that they can gradually be integrated into a modern working environment without any sudden break with their customs. One of the districts receiving his assistance is Quinua, where there are a number of small schools and a kind of central school. In addition, Avemann has established an evening school there which already has ninety adult pupils. Avemann's six textbooks have been made by a simple duplicating procedure. They are not much to look at, but cheap, and they appear to be based on the children's enviroment in such a way as to lead them into the working world instead of away from it. This school district has become a pilot project and five more school districts in the same province have made enquiries about the scheme. The Peruvian Government have indicated their interest in extending the project.

3. MULTILATERAL AID

Twenty-three per cent of government development aid, that is $136 million, passed to developing countries in 1970 through our participation in and contributions to international organisations. First of all there is our participation in the World Bank group, which includes the World Bank and its affiliates the International Finance Corporation (IFC) and the International Development Association (IDA). The task of the Bank group is to help member countries by providing loans. In the financial year 1969-70, the World Bank's loans and investment commitments amounted to $2,300 million. In addition, the Bank exercises a guiding function in the field of development aid, especially as it has meanwhile discarded the narrow concept of economic growth. With 5.02 per cent of the Bank's capital stock of about $23,000 million, the Federal Republic of Germany is one of the three biggest holders, the others being the United States and Britain. The Federal Republic of Germany contributed $243 million towards the $3,230 million available to the IDA between 1960 and 1970 for loans on particularly favourable terms.

The Federal Republic has also provided $34 million of the capital stock of the Asian Development Bank, which provides assistance for Asian countries who are members of the United Nations Economic Commission for Asia and the Far East. Between 1971 and 1974, the Federal Republic of Germany will have provided DM64 million ($18 million) for the Special Fund of the Asian Development Bank. It contributes about 33 per cent of the European Development Fund towards which the six members of the EEC have together contributed $684,000 million under the second Yacundé agreement. The Fund, which is administered by the European Commission, benefits the eighteen African countries south of the Sahara and Madagascar, which have particularly close traditional ties with members of the Community. It can be used for subsidies, credits and capital participations, though up to now it has mainly provided finance for infrastructure projects. In 1971 the Federal Republic of Germany contributed $14 million towards the United Nations Development Programme (UNDP). UNDP provides technical assistance for developing countries through the UN specialised agencies. It is determined by the industrial and the developing countries and in 1971 was worth $300 million.

The Federal Republic of Germany also provides direct grants for the United Nations specialised agencies, most of which benefit the developing countries. The Food and Agriculture Organisation (FAO), for instance, has contributed to the "Green Revolution" with the varieties of wheat and rice it has developed, whilst the International Labour Organisation (ILO) is heavily involved in efforts to provide jobs in the Third World. The United Nations Education, Scientific and Cultural Organisation (UNESCO) is developing new teaching and learning methods that are adapted to conditions in developing countries. The World Health Organisation (WHO) has achieved considerable success with its measures to combat malaria, cholera, yellow fever and other diseases. The other specialised agencies to which the Federal Republic of Germany contributes funds and personnel, such as the United Nations Industrial Development Organisation (UNIDO), are active in the field of development aid. The United Nations International Children's Emergency Fund (UNICEF), which has long since extended its activities beyond charitable programmes, received c. $2 million from the Federal Republic of Germany in 1970.

Since 1970 the Federal Republic of Germany has provided a total of $3 million for the United Nations Fund for Population Activities, whose advisory committee the author of this book was invited to join by the then UN Secretary General U Thant. The Fund, which is administered by the UNDP, has set itself three tasks in the field of family planning. First, it proposes to show how absolutely essential family planning has become. Second, it intends to co-ordinate the efforts already being made by individual governments and the international organisations. And third, it will provide financial support where the will and the organisation are available but not the money.

It is precisely with family planning, where national resentment is more easily aroused than in any other field, that the United Nations has a chance. For this reason the Fund itself should grow faster than any of its activities. There is little distinction between multilateral and bilateral projects, except that individual United Nations agencies have acquired an experience in their fields which the government departments of industrial countries do not always have. The International Labour Organisation, for instance, launched projects aimed at creating employment or stopping the drift from the land at a time when all the world spoke only of growth rates. One such project, which is intended to reach between 6,000 and 8,000 people, was begun in Nigeria in 1969 at a place twenty-five miles north of Lagos. The purpose of the project is to advise farmers on methods of growing maize, rice and cassava and to help them in the processing of their crops to enable them to obtain higher prices. In addition, craftsmen are trained for the building, timber and metalworking trades, and the establishment of co-operatives. School leavers and unemployed young people can also learn a trade. Finally, the people living in the project area are building roads and bridges on a self-help basis.

The interesting point about this project is that it involves the co-operation of various United Nations organisations. Agricultural extension work is in the hands of the FAO, UNICEF is providing the equipment for six workshops (for mechanics, plumbers and carpenters), whereas the ILO is in charge of the whole project. The Nigerian Government provides auxiliary personnel, the land and the buildings for the workshops, as well as accommodation for the experts. The project manager is an Englishman and his deputy is a German, but there is also a Dutch and an Indian expert. The project, which was completed at the end of 1971, has started a development in the Western State which will be passed on and be an encouragment to others.

For a long time opinion in the Federal Republic of Germany tended to be against multilateral aid. We paid because others, particularly the Americans, paid and expected us to make a contribution. But we paid grudgingly under the motto : not one Deutschmark more than necessary. In the meantime many people have recognised that active participation in the international organisations is also of ever-increasing importance for our foreign relations. Multilateral aid is appreciated by the developing countries, and all the more so depending on the extent to which public opinion in these countries is sensitive about bilateral aid. The United States is today switching rapidly to multilateral aid for the simple reason that its bilateral help has brought more trouble than sympathy.

Although this cannot yet be said to apply to German aid, we would surely be well advised to keep on increasing the proportion of multilateral aid we give. The almost academic dispute over the advantages of bilateral and multilateral aid resolves itself : nobody can abandon bilateral aid overnight for the sake of multilateral aid since the international organisations lack the necessary capacity, but nobody will be able to prevent development aid from becoming in the long run politically tolerable only if it is made available by common effort.

4. CAPITAL AID

Capital aid, or loans, has lost some of its significance in spite of the fact that it still accounts for the greater part of our aid contributions. Whereas most of our technical assistance is concentrated in countries where a basis must first be established for the utilisation of capital (in 1970, 46.4 per cent of our technical assistance commitments in the narrower sense of the word went to Africa), most of our capital aid goes to Asia (52.2 per cent of our loan agrements in 1970 were with Asian countries, in particular India, Pakistan, Indonesia and Turkey).

Most credits are intended for the development of infrastructure : roads, railways, bridges, ports, airports, dams and water supply systems. The proportion of capital aid for factories is declining, and that still provided is used for the production of fertilisers, textiles or sugar. Approximately one tenth of this aid is disbursed through development banks. A considerable proportion takes the form of commodity aid, usually supplies of raw materials and spare parts for existing industrial plant.

In Germany some people think we give money which anybody can make use of or not as he sees fit, but in the recipient countries they tend to complain about the laborious procedure from the initial application for aid until work actually begins, and about the all too large numbers of preliminary and feasibility studies before the *Kreditanstalt für Wiederaufbau* (Development Loan Corporation) is authorised by the inter-ministerial committee to go ahead with the disbursement procedure. German administrative departments are accused of taking too much rather than too little care.

In the early years our economists believed that interest rates should be such as to induce sound financial policies in developing countries also. This, at any rate, was the explanation for the high rates of interest charged in the early sixties which were partly responsible for the serious indebtedness of some developing countries. But in 1969 it was the Federal Republic of Germany which advocated in the CECD that the developing countries should be given better terms, and since then our credits have usually been granted at 2.5 per cent interest for periods of thirty years with eight years of grace. Comparing this with market conditions, this means that two-thirds of it was a gift. Aid-tying, that is, insisting that loans granted be used to purchase goods in the Federal Republic of Germany, is a practice that is quickly being abandoned (from 57 per cent in 1967 to 26 per cent in 1970) because the developing countries receive on average 20 per cent less value than they do for untied aid, for in the latter case the firms submitting tenders are open to international competition.

Quite a number of capital aid projects are being implemented in Tunisia, a country which suffers from having sometimes too little water through drought and at others too much through floods. One financial assistance project has been started with a view to protecting the city of Tunis from the floods. Only in 1964 the Miliane river flooded an area of 35 sq. miles, including the southern parts of the capital, and caused $5 million worth of damage. When the floods came again in 1969 construction of the dam had reached such an advanced stage that the amount of damage to it, which was covered by insurance, remained within limits.

Today it is half an hour's drive from Tunis to the south-west along a Roman aqueduct to the Bir M'Cherga Dam near the Roman town of Thuburbo Majus. It is 1,500 yards long and can hold up to 200 million cubic metres of water and allow it to flow evenly. From a 420 ft. high tower water can be drawn from different depths to establish the saline content, for, and this is one of Tunisia's problems, this water, too, is salty. Now efforts are being made to channel off the less salty flows of water, to mix them with better water, and use it for irrigation on the Cap Bon peninsula. This project, which has been executed by a French firm of consulting engineers and a German contractor working under Tunisian management and involving about $4 million capital aid from Germany, would be worth it even if it only put a stop to the flooding, but that will certainly not be the only effect.

5. OTHER FORMS OF ASSISTANCE

The scope of this book does not permit me to expound on all the different kinds of assistance provided and all the various instruments of official development aid ranging from trainee programmes (up to the end of 1970 about 51,000 specialists from developing countries had been trained in the Federal Republic of Germany, most of them counterparts who eventually take over from our experts) via help in improving social structures which directly benefits the underprivileged, to trade aid designed to give exporters in developing countries easier access to German markets. Similarly, it would require too much space to give details about the contributions made by the Churches and private organisations, such as the Kübel Foundation, which have been outstanding both in quality and quantity. Nor is this the place to describe the work of the German Foundation for Developing Countries with its four centres for information, industrial training, agriculture and administration, nor the efforts of the political foundations (the Friedrich Ebert Foundation, the Konrad Adenauer Foundation, the Friedrich Naumann Foundation) in advising trade unions, co-operatives and other groups, nor, in particular, the extensive activities of the German Volunteer Service (DED), which to many of my countrymen is synonymous with personnel aid.

But perhaps it is appropriate to say something about the variety of these instruments, especially as one constantly hears the demand for more light to be shed on the jungle of organisations administering development aid. As long as each organisation sticks to its own particular task then there can be no objection to having such a variety. Trainee courses for personnel from developing countries, which are organised by the Carl Duisberg Society, are not the same as preparing German experts for their assignments abroad. Seminars for top-level personnel from developing countries (such as the ones arranged by the German Foundation in Berlin) are different from the seminars on social affairs organised by the Friedrich Ebert Foundation in La Catalina (Costa Rica). And the promotion of private investment by the German Development Company in Cologne is different from the research work of the Development Institute in Berlin.

As long as overlapping and disputes over competence can be prevented there are advantages in variety. It is an obstacle to the formation of mammoth institutions. Individual organisations are more mobile abroad if they are not seen as government functionaries and it is easier for them to make contact with related groups.

Within the ambit of development aid it is mostly societies rather than government agencies which come into contact, and it would be neither fitting nor beneficial for our society to present itself as a structure more integrated and uniform than it actually is. Thus I feel the task of government departments, especially the Federal Ministry for Economic Co-operation, lies not in the achievement of uniformity but in the management, delimitation and co-ordination of aid measures.

It could be argued that a volunteer service such as the DED sometimes causes irritation when it adopts resolutions that are not compatible with the Federal Government's policy. The answer is that democracy is altogether a strenuous business and that in most industrial countries there can only be a volunteer service which is in many respects independent or there can be none at all. Of course, it is not a good thing for small organisations to want to build up their own machinery, but variety in the organisation of development aid derives not merely from the diversity of the tasks involved but also from the plurality of our society.

6. PRIVATE INVESTMENT

In recent years no subject has caused tempers to flare as much as that of private investment in developing countries. This is in spite of the fact that not even the terminology is clear. Private direct investment by German firms is not the same thing as the "private capital transfers" referred to in OECD statistics. The latter include medium-term commercial export credits as well as borrowings by the World Bank or the regional development banks in the German capital market. It also includes portfolio investments, i.e., the acquisition of holdings in developing countries, which, in 1969 for instance, accounted for more than two and a half times the amount of private direct investment.

All the same, even though direct German investment in developing countries is much less than many people assume, and though it is equivalent to only just over half of French, one third of British, and one ninth of American investment, and less than one third of the official development aid provided so far, and even if the proportion of investment in developing countries has for years run to no more than 30 per cent of total foreign investment by German industry, it is worth examining this type of capital transfer, especially as its importance in relation to official aid is increasing.

In the Federal Republic of Germany, too, there are two rigidly opposed schools of thought : those who consider direct investment to be the best form of development aid in any event and those who regard it merely as neo-colonialist exploitation. The one side feel that everything that is profitable is justifiable in terms of development policy, whilst to the other side it is precisely the profit which is the unmistakable mark of capitalist exploitation. In reality it is surely that not everything profitable from a company point of view is right in terms of development policy for that reason alone, but no investment which does not also benefit the national economy can help a developing country.

This leads us to search for criteria that are the subject of research by various German and international teams (i.e. within the OECD). What is the effect of private investment on employment and unemployment, on the balance of payments situation, the national budget, the regional economic structure, the spread of income and consumer habits? What proportion of the profits are re-invested in the country and what proportion transferred to the industrial country? How many young people receive training and how much know-how is transferred? Is the enterprise integrated into the economic structure or does it remain a foreign body? Are local partners (private and public) involved? Is there any chance of the enterprise passing into local hands (a majority holding) after a certain period of time? Is production oriented to the needs of a small minority or to those of the mass of the population? To what extent is production a burden on the environment?

Of course, these are not the criteria upon which an

enterprise will base its decision whether or not to invest. An expert of the Confederation of German Industry put it this way : "Investment in developing countries is definitely not motivated by development aid; nevertheless such investment generates impulses which are important for the economic development of the country concerned".[56] To make sure that the right kind of impulse will ensue, many developing countries have drawn up their own policies. Countries like India, Algeria, Peru and Colombia are quite specific about the kind of investment they want and do not want, and what is in their interest and what is not. Most of them want to achieve rapid economic and social progress in accordance with their own direction. For this they require foreign capital and know-how, but not at any price and on any terms.

Placing trade surpluses at their disposal free of charge will not help them in itself because the trade gap will exist for a long time to come. There is only a very limited amount of official development aid available, even if one day it actually does reach the target of 0.7 per cent of industrial countries' GNP. If only for the sake of raising total net capital flows to one per cent of the latter's GNP—and this is the minimum demanded by developing countries—commercial imports of capital will be indispensable. As regards direct investments, there is the additional consideration that along with them goes a flow of technical and organisational know-how.

For this reason most developing countries prefer direct foreign investment and encourage it in various ways. However, they always make the point that their sovereignty and development plans have priority and that only within this framework is it possible to find an equitable balance of interests. This is a theme which recurs in both national and international documents, ranging from the recommendations adopted by the United Nations Conference on Trade and Development in 1964 via the Charter of Algiers and the declarations of the Latin American states made at Vina del Mar in 1969, to the United Nations Strategy Document adopted in October 1970.

On the other hand, the investment policies of individual countries, such as Indonesia, Ghana or Argentina, follow a zig-zag course by comparison. Yet there is a certain trend, a tendency to fix the terms, to direct investment along policy lines, and to take a close and critical look at the long-term costs and benefits of direct investment. There are inconsistencies in the practice of granting concessions, there are ideological prejudices and demagogic manoeuvres if a whipping-boy is wanted to satisfy opinion at home, and there are sham arrangements, such as partnerships with dummy companies. But investors would be short-sighted if, on account of this, they lost sight of this trend. There is no point in keeping a black list and moving to those countries with a particularly liberal investment policy. Naturally, unnecessary risks have to be avoided, but we should learn from the experience of the North Americans and the history of oil concessions that a liberal investment policy is no life insurance and that centrally controlled, nationalistic or socialist investment policies do not by any means exclude the possibility of profitable investment. Many German enterprises recognised this long ago, and some are finding this out with, of all countries, our Eastern neighbours.

All this is more laborious and complicated than the good old-fashioned investment of colonial days. But in the East and the South there is an unsatiated demand for capital and know-how which someone or other will come forward to meet, although he cannot ask the prices and make the profits originally envisaged. Comparable partners are hard to find; this we know from the difficulties encountered by the German Development Company. In the long term we cannot get round the fact that in many developing countries only public or semi-public enterprises can seriously be considered as partners for German firms. This may or may not have disadvantages but it reduces the political risks.

Most developing countries, by no means only those who believe in the capitalist economy, do not at all have the impression that too much is being invested in their countries. On the contrary, they offer tax incentives, pass special laws and regulations, issue licences, set up agencies, and establish development banks and industrial estates. They improve vocational training systems, roads and power supply systems, and they launch publicity campaigns. Yet the investors stay away or else there are so few of them it is hardly worthwhile. Or in some cases their approach is different to what has been expected or their activities have proved to be a failure. Or else foreign investors make the same mistake as their local counterparts : they flock into overcrowded areas such as São Paulo, Buenos Aires or Mexico City.

This is certainly not the fault of the investors alone but is often due to the inability of the developing countries to direct and utilise investment properly. Effective planning and guidance of the investment process by the government concerned are in the interest of foreign investors. They need clear information, reliable subcontractors, and stable markets. A clear, hard line is better for them than the patchwork of arbitrary interventions. The developing countries have long enough pinned their hopes to the magical power of the market machinery which by allowing for complete competition does all the guiding for them. The markets and the structure of the developing countries are much further away from achieving this aim than ours are. We had therefore better avoid transferring to them our own economic policy patterns. Indeed, it is in our own interest to help the developing countries plan and direct investment activities.

What the Federal Government can do to guide investment is of only secondary consideration. Nobody in the

Federal Republic of Germany can tell a company where and how it should invest. The only question is which investments should be promoted from public funds—including tax concessions. My view that our promotion instruments need improvement and can be improved is meanwhile well known. This criticism is based on the results of scientific studies.

1. We can see from the regional distribution of direct German investments in developing countries that nearly 77 per cent (as at 31 December 1970) of these investments were effected in Latin America or in European developing countries. Within the individual regions they have been concentrated on the more progressive countries.

2. Thus promotional instruments are of secondary importance when investors come to make their decisions. What matters most are the expected profits and the size of the market.

3. The promotional instruments are mostly used by big enterprises that least require assistance for projects which would be attractive enough without financial support.

4. Assistance generally depends on whether the project is "worthy of promotion", but there are not the criteria for effectively applying this principle when decisions are made, nor the practical means.

So it is quite clear that perfectionist promotional measures with a high administrative input help nobody. But tax concessions could, for instance, be limited to investments in what really are developing countries, and to processing industries. (It is mostly investment in the extractive rather than the processing sector that is held up as an example of exploitation.) And perhaps it would be possible to agree with some governments that certain densely populated areas in their countries will not be considered for promotion.

It seems there is a growing willingness among our

industrial firms to discuss a more definite set of instruments which will be aligned to the needs of the developing countries. Moreover, it is to be hoped that the criticism of private investment will be more specific and based not so much on ideological generalisations as on verifiable shortcomings.

V Tasks

1. The Role of the Federal Republic of Germany

THE DEVELOPMENT aid contributions of the Federal Republic of Germany, which were begun out of political considerations, then intensified with a view to achieving economic aims, today play an important role. According to statistics published by the OECD, only the United States total transfers in 1969 exceeded those of the Federal Republic of Germany. In 1970 Japan and France overtook the Federal Republic, which now occupies fourth place in the OECD list of donors. The position may have changed again in 1971, especially as private flows fluctuate according to economic activity and interest rates.

The Federal Republic of Germany is not a superpower. Unlike the United States and the Soviet Union, it has no sphere of influence to defend. It is too small to play the part of the world's policeman. Ever since the adoption of the Monroe Doctrine, the United States has felt itself responsible for the Western hemisphere and its commitments in Latin America do not represent a new development. In South East Asia and in the Middle East its interests clash with those of the Soviet Union. To the great powers development aid was part of defence policy, or in some cases a vehicle for helping to establish a certain ideology.

France and Britain have carried on their traditional relations with their former colonies. The Germans, late on the scene as a nation-state, were also slow to emerge as an imperialistic power, at a time when this gave to conflict with other European powers. The end of the first world war was also the end of the brief spell of German colonial history. The painful process of decolonisation was an experience which the Germans did not have to go through for we lost our colonies just in time. As a result, German development aid could not fall back on the experience of the former colonial administrations. On top of this, there is the language barrier. The spread of French culture has shaped the development of many African countries, whereas German is not an official language in any country of the Third World and it is hardly taught or spoken there. The Scandinavian countries also had no colonial traditions or pretensions to being world powers. To social democratic Sweden development aid was a natural dictate of humanitarianism. No hatred had built up against these countries and their aid was not suspected of being a new means of continuing colonial domination. Much the same opportunity was open to the Federal Republic. Yet the more the Federal Republic's claim to be the sole representative of the German nation was seen to be the motive for its development aid and the more its economic strength increased, the more the developing countries were inclined to suspect that it, too, had neo-colonialist intentions. The Federal Republic of Germany provides development aid to all regions of the world, the only country apart from the United States to do so. It is easy to make enemies with development aid; making friends is a much more difficult task.

Wherever peace is discussed in the world today it soon becomes linked with the name of Willy Brandt. The Chancellor of the Federal Republic of Germany is seen as one of the few statesmen to have realised what is required today : to direct the energy of mankind to the fulfilment of those tasks on which everybody's future depends. This may be one of the reasons why many developing countries look to the Federal Republic. Another is probably the fact that the Federal Republic, which has fewer Cabinet ministers than any of its predecessors and many of its neighbours, has not only retained the federal ministry responsible for development aid but given it additional responsibilities. The decision taken by the Cabinet on 11 February 1971 was particularly impressive and has evoked admiration in many quarters.

2. Orientation of Aid to the Targets of the Developing Countries

On 11 February 1971, the Federal Government adopted its Development Policy Concept for the second development decade. This is the first time the public have been given a full survey of the aims, principles, programmes and methods of development policy. This document defines the role of development aid in the Federal Republic's overall policy and states that the economic and social progress of the developing countries is also in the interest of the Federal Republic of Germany, both from the economic and the foreign policy point of view: "Economically, this creates the preconditions for an expanded exchange of goods and services in the interests of both sides." And in terms of foreign relations: "Effective development policy strengthens the international position of the Federal Republic of Germany. In the long term it increases the chances of securing peace. Development policy, therefore, fits into the overall policy of the Federal Republic of Germany and into the network of its foreign relations", but it is "of no value as an instrument of short-term foreign policy considerations".

Official development aid provided by the Federal Republic of Germany should, according to the Cabinet decision, be oriented to the aims and priorities of the developing countries. It is by no means a matter of fact that policies should not merely serve national interests but endeavour "constantly to balance the interests of all concerned", in other words those of industrial and developing countries, so that the aims of other countries are explicitly recognised as a guideline. The policy concept proposes that this balance should be achieved within a system of world-wide partnership in which the independence of the developing countries is fully respected. "The Federal Government is not seeking to impose its own political, social or economic policy ideas on the developing countries. In close co-operation with the country concerned and with other aid-givers, it decides which measures it will support according to its possibilities, its ideas and its instruments of aid."

If one considers that German development aid was at one time intended as a means of spreading the gospel of the free market economy, then this is really saving something. Development aid is no longer a vehicle for exporting an ideology that will resolve everybody's problems but an attempt to help others find their own way, even if it is not our own. But this also means that development aid can only be secondary to the efforts of the developing countries themselves. But what are the aims of the developing countries? Who formulates them and for whose benefit? Has the Federal Government no aims of its own? Development aid cannot be used to further every aim, of course, no matter who defines it or where it leads to. Nobody will deny that there is exploitation and oppression in developing countries, but no one will expect the Federal Government to support it.

Thus we have the rare case of the problem being more difficult to solve in theory than in practice. Considering the large number of applications and requests for aid, the Federal Government must in any case choose between them. If only because funds are always limited, it is necessary to select only those projects which at least do not conflict with our own ideas of development. Projects merely designed to build up the prestige of a political leader have no more chance of being promoted than those which benefit only a small upper class.

The fact that we give preference to projects which

benefit those who need help most is not inconsistent with our intention of orienting aid to the aims of the developing countries. We cannot force any government to accept a project it does not want. Similarly, no one can compel us to finance a project that is not in keeping with our own principles. We shall always try to incorporate our aims as harmoniously as possible in the plans of the developing countries. But where we do so we will have to decide according to our own criteria.

3. DEVELOPMENT POLICY AND OUR OWN INTERESTS

Effective development policy must be guarded and asserted against two factions: those who see it as a welcome opportunity to put small favours in the way of German firms or foreign governments, and those who condemn any link between development aid and other interests as disreputable. There has never been such a thing as politics completely dissociated from interests, and there never will be. And in the case of development policy also it is not a question of denying our interests but of understanding them and defining them.

Capital aid and exports

Whoever intends to promote exports by means of capital aid should start from the following facts:

1. In 1970 capital aid accounted for one per cent of our exports.

2. As long as our economy remains competitive a large proportion of this relatively small sum will in any case be spent in the Federal Republic. It is the big firms (especially those in the electrical and building branches) who receive most of the orders. From the point of view of export promotion, capital aid is by no means a bonus for firms making highly competitive offers; indeed, what counts is the firm's presence and skilful tactics in the country concerned and in Bonn.

In the view of an expert who has been concerned with the practical and theoretical aspects of development problems for many years, development aid brings only indirect and long-term economic benefit to the donor countries.[57] A development policy aimed at deriving the greatest possible benefit for developing countries is therefore the most likely means of serving our own long-term economic interests.

It is a well-known fact that industrial countries mostly cultivate trade with other industrial countries. This trade produces the biggest growth rates and the greater benefits of a world-wide division of labour. Consequently, the more the developing countries proceed towards industrialisation, the greater the possibilities for expanding trade and the greater the benefits to be derived by all concerned from the universal division of labour. This is particularly important for the Federal Republic of Germany since a substantial proportion of its gross national product comes from foreign trade.[58]

A country which, for the sake of short-term export advantages, does not design its development policy to contribute as much as possible to economic and social progress in the developing countries is only harming its own economy in the long run. Furthermore, the detachment of German development policy from short-term German export interests (and which are only partial ones at that) is not incompatible with our own economic aims. If only because of the long process between the actual application for assistance and the time when the first monetary transfers are made, development aid could only in exceptional cases have an anti-cyclical effect. Development aid cannot, therefore, be used as an instrument of cyclical policy.

Development aid and structural policy

A growth-oriented structural policy makes it easier to phase out firms and industries which find themselves on the border-lines of productivity and profitability.

This is done by "active development" and the promotion of growth industries. The process of industrialisation in the developing countries runs parallel to this. There is an increase in those branches of industry in which the developing countries are relatively productive in comparison to the industrial countries. In the latter, on the other hand, new highly productive industries emerge as a result of the rapid advance of technology. Industries that have become relatively unproductive tie down scarce resources and hamper the future-oriented sectors.

A combined development and structural policy can facilitate this process, perhaps by providing for the abandonment of unproductive industries and their transfer to developing countries. It could also help avoid the risk of funds being misdirected through the grant of subsidies for unproductive industries and protectionism against emerging competition from developing countries. To promote their industrialisation the developing countries have started to process their own raw materials. Certain low levels of processing will disappear in the industrial countries since instead of being supplied with the raw materials they need they will be offered larger quantities of processed commodities (e.g. finished rather than crude copper, etc.). Protectionist measures and subsidies designed to prevent the transfer of these initial levels of processing to the developing countries are bound to fail in the long run.

Development policy and foreign policy

Development policy is not a suitable vehicle for the attainment of short-term foreign policy objectives. As a general rule, it cannot influence the foreign policy of the developing country to suit the purposes of the donor country. "Aid for development does not usually buy dependable friends."[59] With these words the Pearson Commission says that development aid cannot normally prevent the developing countries from pursuing their own foreign policy, not even if it runs contrary to the (short-term) interests of the donor country. The experience of the Americans in this respect speaks a clear language, and American contributions are much less marginal than the German.

The tying of American foreign aid to American security interests has in many cases if anything harmed American foreign policy objectives. On account of this policy new governments assuming power in developing countries have often ruthlessly broken off all relations with the United States and turned for assistance to its adversary. If United States development policy had been detached from foreign and defence policy the reaction would not have been so violent. This is also the view taken by the Pearson Commission.[60]

Development policy aimed at short-term foreign policy objectives is a threat to medium and long-term relations with the developing countries. The instruments of development policy are only effective on a long-term basis since the planning and execution of projects and programmes usually takes many years. Foreign policy, on the other hand, must frequently be adjusted to sudden changes (e.g. an unexpected change of government).[61] Development policy which gives priority to the objectives pursued by the developing countries over short-term German interests will in the long run benefit our foreign policy.

Again, a development policy governed by the interests of aid-givers cannot bring the optimum benefit for the developing countries. If project decisions are based on such criteria the funds are in many cases used ineffectively. A project that has not been adapted to the country's needs can be a heavy burden because it uses up already scarce funds which could be put to more appropriate use.[62] Development projects which the government of a developing country is persuaded to adopt even though they are out of place both economically and technologically may mean big orders for export firms in the industrial country, but relations with that country are more likely to deteriorate after a short time.

The Pearson Commission arrives at the following conclusion: "A good deal of bilateral aid has indeed been dispensed in order to achieve short-term political favors, gain strategic advantages, or promote exports from the donor...It is hardly surprising therefore that hopes of satisfactory development progress were disappointed."[63] Word of this gets round in the developing countries also. Development policy subordinated to the short-term interests of the donor country is a help to neither side; indeed it is apt to strain relations. Development policy serving short-term interests leads to disappointments. This has already become unmistakably clear in the United States, as indicated by the study on United States development aid, which reads: "Foreign aid in its present form is an insult, at home and abroad."[64] As a result of the crisis in relations between the United States and the developing countries, official aid has been greatly reduced, by about one half between 1963 and 1969,[65] but this is not likely to make things better.

Where development aid is expected to bring direct economic, political or even military advantages it ends up in crisis as soon as it is realised that these advantages are not forthcoming. And they cannot materialise since at least the younger generation in the developing countries do not regard development aid as benevolent alms-giving but as part compensation for flagrant injustice—and paltry compensation at that. Thus bitterness spreads, and this bitterness is given as the argument for reducing aid contributions, and these smaller contributions build up discontent in the developing countries. Here we are threatened with an escalation of discontent which will develop into a first-rate political issue.

President Nixon's message to Congress on 15 September 1970 shows that the American administration has recognised this danger. It is therefore making a last-minute attempt to throw the helm over, by drawing a strict division between military and development aid and by shifting the emphasis to multilateral aid. The fact that the Americans are now reverting to methods and tendencies which have been evident in the Federal Republic of Germany for some time now is no cause for complacency, but we do in fact have a good chance of avoiding the escalation of discontent.

It is a thoroughly legitimate interest of the Federal Republic of Germany to make friends through development aid and at least not to make enemies. In this respect the positive and the negative possibilities are greater than we are usually prepared to admit. Naive as it may be to hope to win a country's special sympathy by providing a power station or a technical school, it is none the less certain that the overall picture of development aid in our relations with the Third World cannot be valued too highly. The constructive part which the German delegation played in the work of the Preparatory Committee for the second development decade was of political significance, as was the Federal Government's advocacy of a reduction in the normal interest rate and of the discontinuance of the practice of aid tying. And so was the fact that the Federal Republic became the second largest contributor to the multilateral organisations after the United States, made it possible for IDA's funds to be generously increased, and played an active part in UNESCO's development aid programmes. The response was favourable, and in 1970 the German candidate for the Executive Board of UNESCO surprisingly obtained 94 of the 119 votes.

And political significance will also attach to the Federal Republic's efforts to achieve the United Nations target of 0.7 per cent of GNP in the form of official aid. The developing countries would be interested to see whether the Federal Republic of Germany, where it is a question of rescheduling their debts, will be applying the brake or whether it will itself take an active part. The developing countries will note whether in future we claim our full quota of credits at higher interest rates as conceded by the OECD, whether we increase our educational aid, whether the training and adaptability of our experts improves, and what influence the German Forum for Development Policy will exercise on German public opinion.

In short, it is in our own interest to pursue a good and effective development policy. It is also in our interest to orient our policy to the aims of the developing countries and the United Nations Strategy Document for the second decade. Nobody will be able to tell for certain whether a good development policy will bring political compensation, but in any event it opens up the opportunity for partnership which can also bear political fruit. One of the unpleasant experiences of recent years has been that poor, short-sighted development aid distorted by sectional interests and either given as a reward or denied the developing country because it has incurred the donor's displeasure is worthless. Development aid is an investment in a common future in so far as we really mean the common future. Our partners are quick to sense this.

4. The New Concept

The common future was also the criterion applied when the United Nations Strategy Document for the second development decade was drafted. And it was the yardstick for the Development Policy Concept adopted by the German Federal Government on 11 February 1971. Where it is a question of meeting the needs of the population the areas of concentration are obvious—education, employment and food. In the rather dry language of a Cabinet decision, this reads as follows on agriculture[66] :

"In most developing countries during the second

development decade, the agricultural sector will remain decisive for improving the living conditions of the majority of the population. This makes it important for German development aid.

"Successes in the sector of agricultural production ('Green Revolution') have made it clear that the bottle-necks are to be found primarily in the lack of purchasing power of the poorer sections of the population as well as in the forward and backward linkage sectors.

"Social tensions have in many cases been aggravated by the 'Green Revolution'. For this reason, promotion measures in the agricultural sector will only become fully effective in many countries when promising agricultural reforms are launched. The Federal Government considers such measures important and is ready to support them.

"In the future, the instruments of agricultural aid will be applied preferably where they are able to contribute to the success of sound agricultural structural measures taken by the developing countries. This will require the increased secondment of government advisers as well as the promotion of credit, procurement, production and marketing organisations. Above all the development of extension services and agricultural credit systems will be promoted. The promotion of agricultural research and technology is to be intensified. There will be increased on-the-spot co-operation between highly qualified advisers and research workers and the relevant institutions in the developing countries.

"In the production sector, special attention is to be given to animal and vegetable protein production. In the processing sectors, the storage, marketing, distribution and processing of agricultural products are gaining increasing importance. Here, special account is to be taken of the possibilities of exporting processed and manufactured products.

"The Federal Republic of Germany will promote the rational manufacture of agricultural production requisites in the developing countries. This will also include the setting up of efficient repair and advisory services. These factors are to be taken into account when production requisites are supplied.

"Greater emphasis is to be given to on-the-spot training and further training of senior personnel as well as medium-grade technical and organisational personnel; training is also to be geared as much as possible to practical requirements.

"The various promotional measures should be integrated within the framework of larger projects and programmes."

This sector takes up only one page of the thirty-page document, but a whole book could be written on the subject. The dry, concise sentence : "In the future the instruments of agricultural aid will be applied preferably where they are able to contribute to the success of sound agricultural structural measures taken by the developing countries" contains a full programme which, if implemented in minute detail, could set things in motion. And another chapter, on employment[67] :

"The Federal Government will pay increased attention to the effects of its promotional measures on employment, and give support to meaningful employment measures within the framework of regional structural programmes. It will take employment-intensive sectors especially into account.

"In most of the developing countries, urbanisation is taking place more quickly than the demand for labour in industrial agglomerations rises. For this reason, jobs must be created, especially in rural regions. The Federal Government will give increased promotion to labour-intensive sectors of the agricultural economy and the expansion of rural infrastructure.

"The Federal Government will support the development of labour-intensive and at the same time competitive production methods. Also the assuming of local currency costs can contribute to capital and foreign exchange-intensive technologies not being favoured unilaterally. However, labour-intensive production procedures can only be applied, especially in the export industry sector, if the production costs that arise are in keeping with competition on the international markets. The promotion of small and medium-sized undertakings, the building sector and labour-intensive branches of the processing industries will contribute to improved employment both in rural regions and in industrial agglomerations.

"The promotional measures of the Federal Government in the services sector will be designed to help expand labour-intensive services (for example, tourism and public services).

"Direct effects on employment and at the same time improvement in the living conditions of the population can be attained through the promotion of social services. In this respect, self-help organisations, youth, volunteer and work services have an important function, above all in the sector of community development. The Federal Government will, therefore, give increased support to suitable organisations and programmes in this sector.

"The employment policies of the developing countries cannot succeed without a labour and environment-oriented educational system for the mass of the population. The extension of educational aid will, therefore, be increasingly determined by its effects on employment."

Nobody reading this passage cursorily can appreciate the years of inter-ministerial discussions that have gone into the drafting of, say, the following short sentence : "Also the assuming of local currency costs can contribute to capital and foreign-exchange intensive technologies not being favoured unilaterally." From the very beginning it has been a principle of German capital aid to assume costs incurred in foreign exchange rather than in the currency of the developing country. And there were good reasons for this, particularly with regard to the balance of payments situation of the developing country. The disadvantage was that with this we could set up only the kind of plant that is customary in hard-currency countries—that is, as capital-intensive and labour-saving as possible. However, this did not have the desired effect on employment. Occasionally an ultra-modern factory put more small craftsmen out of work than it employed. Thus it is now necessary to assume a larger proportion of local currency costs. There is no reason why a road-building project requiring several thousand local workers should be less eligible for promotion than a similar project using the latest machinery. And finally the chapter on education and science :[68]

"In keeping with the recommendations and programmes of the multilateral organisations, the Federal Government will take into account in the second development decade the importance of education and science for all sectors of development through greater qualitative and quantitative efforts. Promotional measures should aim at a flexible adjustment of education syllabuses and methods to the changing demands of the labour market and the social environment. Effective measures towards structural changes in the educational system and the development of new teaching and learning methods have priority over contributions effecting merely the quantitative expansion of existing educational systems.

"Educational and scientific aid will enjoy an increasing proportion of the growth of technical assistance. In suitable cases, capital aid should also be allocated for investment in this sector.

"Increased support should be given to the following

fields in educational and scientific aid : educational administration, planning and research, measures outside the traditional school system including the use of mass media, flexible vocational education systems, material infrastructure in the educational system, and application-oriented research.

"Scientific aid concentrated up to now on university institutions and application-oriented scientific institutions will be expanded in order to promote basic research in selected spheres of special significance for development.

"Educational and scientific aid will utilize all the possibilities of co-operation in the spirit of partnership between institutions in the developing countries and in the Federal Republic of Germany. In this co-operation, priority is to be given to the requirements of the developing countries. In particular in the provision of educational aid, the indiscriminate transfer of German educational models is to be avoided."

Here, too, one short sentence embraces a whole programme : "Promotional measures should aim at a flexible adjustment of education syllabuses and methods to the changing demands of the labour market and the social environment." This is the end of a form of educational aid based on the assumption that all that is needed is more schools and universities. The fact that it is now possible to use capital aid for educational investment also may mean little to the outsider, but in actual fact we have broken with a time-honoured principle. The real departure in this Cabinet decision lies elsewhere, however. Up to then the Federal Government had always waited for the developing country to submit its applications and then decided on each project after thorough examination. The result was that even good single projects often remained ineffective. In future individual projects will be an exception.[69]

"In the future, development policy decisions are to be taken more than previously on the basis of country-related aid programmes which make it possible to take greater account of differentiation among the developing countries, to determine priorities for projects, to group the numerous isolated individual projects into a consistent programme, and to better coordinate the efforts of the industrial and developing countries. For this reason, country-related aid programmes will be strengthened within the overall framework of German development policy."

In which regions and sectors our instruments can most effectively be applied must first be established by means of country-related aid programme for which purpose all information on the country concerned (e.g. reports of the World Bank and especially the country's development plans) will be collected and evaluated. Only thus can we find out where we can apply our aid to the best effect. After that our instruments (grants, loans, material and personnel aid) will no longer be used individually but in combinations. Where an agricultural co-operative is to be established steps must be taken to ensure that products can be further processed and brought to market. This may perhaps require a small factory, a road or an irrigation system. The children who cannot be absorbed by the co-operative must be trained as craftsmen. And finally a medical station may be included, headed if possible by someone who knows something about family planning.

Such programmes are more successful the more they are incorporated in the national plans of developing countries and the more these plans are co-ordinated with those of the international organisations. In some developing countries it was a popular sport to play off industrial countries and international organisations against one another. In the meantime many have realised that little can be achieved by this policy and that it is better to co-ordinate help from outside in such a way as to avoid friction and duplication of work and to ensure that functions are suitably distributed. Since the conference of Heidelberg in June 1970, the idea of international co-ordination on the spot, i.e. in the developing country itself, has gained much ground. This is also the aim of revising the UNDP so that the Programme's representatives can become the nucleus of co-ordination measures. On this point the German Cabinet decision reads as follows :[70]

"The achievement of the development policy concept for the seventies depends decisively on co-operation and co-ordination between bilateral and multilateral donors, as well as on the dialogue with the developing countries. The co-ordination of the various bilateral and multilateral aids with the demands of development plans and the requirements of the individual developing countries and a closer connection with the overall system of the United Nations is indispensable.

"In the programming of multilateral aid and the co-ordination of multilateral and bilateral aid, special importance must be attached, within the scope of their responsibilities, to the multilateral organisations which are permanently represented at the country level. For the effective co-ordination of the various aid contributions, better information about projects and programmes is needed. The Federal Government feels that the development and expansion of effective information systems in the developing countries would be useful. This would include, among other things, the establishment of central information offices which store and process project and planning-related data and make it available on request to the bilateral and multilateral donors. Efforts to create an integrated system of information within the UN organisations are supported by the Federal Government. Also the efforts of the World Bank to expand its programme of country missions, to extend their assignments and to co-operate more closely with the UN Development Programme (UNDP) and the IMF in the exchange of information will help to further improve the situation in the matter of information and co-ordination.

"The Federal Government will support all measures leading to more effective co-ordination of aid programmes among bilateral and multilateral donors and with the developing countries. One way to do this is through concerted dialogue on the spot."

Of course, it will be some time before the "concerted dialogue on the spot" gets under way in some countries. And it will require a great deal of tact and judgment to convince the developing countries that this dialogue contains not a danger but an opportunity for them to recruit the help of powerful nations for their own plans. And this also resolves the dispute over bilateral and multilateral aid. Bilateral aid can be applied most effectively in a multilateral framework. It is obvious that such a transition to "long-term, integrated, country-related and internationally co-ordinated aid programmes"[71] calls for organisational changes. For this purpose the Federal Ministry for Economic Co-operation was reorganised in the autumn of 1970. The sections responsible for aid to different countries were increased from 7 to 11 and they prepare the programmes, whilst the sections dealing with the various types of aid elaborate and supervise projects. This reorganisation has also affected those agencies responsible for the implementation of technical assistance projects.

5. SOCIAL STRUCTURES AND DEVELOPMENT POLICY

Today it is nearly everywhere recognised that the aim of social change is to remove obstacles to the mobilisation of self-help and the equitable distribution of its rewards. And there is general agreement in theory where it is a question of villages in the bush, the slums of big cities, migrant workers or orphans, but the situation is different when changes start to interfere with power-relationships. The wind of change now blowing over our planet will in the long run leave no corner of any society untouched. But nobody knows what will be left after it has passed over. Liberation movements aimed at establishing centrally governed states and invoking socialist models appear to know the right answer. Many point to the indisputable successes of Communist China. But although it is well that we should not measure Mao's methods by West European standards it would surely be naïve to paint all societies with the same brush. There can be no dogmatically uniform recipe. We cannot describe the objectives of social change with the concepts and ideas taken from the teachings of one or the other ideology. We must remain overt, and this also means co-operating with states which have dubious systems if they are capable of taking the country forward. A sound tax system, land reform and taking power out of the hands of the parasitic sections of society can also give further help where the grounds are purely nationalistic. What matters most is not so much the motives as the effects. To me development policy is the art of supporting pragmatic changes and in so doing not to destroy what little in the way of order and systematic communications between states and communities was left behind after colonialism and world wars. Conversely, those who believe they are capable of preventing change, be it social or political, may, through their obsession with maintaining order, very quickly end up not only in inhumanity but also in disorder. Pakistan is an example of this.

I have never entered into the theoretical discussion on whether social change should be brought about with or without the use of force. Apart from the fact that the concept of force has meanwhile been widened to such an extent that it appears to imply any form of power, I would simply say that the impulse for most social change over the past ten years or so has come not from guerillas but by revolutionary officers or—as in India, Ceylon and China—from free elections. Amateurish attempts to use force are more apt to consolidate rather than change existing structures and the events of 1971 indicate that there is another alternative to change with or without the use of force: force without change ensuing. I am afraid that this alternative, the effects of which we have seen in Pakistan and Turkey, and in Ceylon and Morocco, will probably become so frequently applied that an all too romantic partiality for force will not last long.

But what can we do if we can neither start, nor want to start, a revolution for others? How can development aid influence social structures? Nobody can say with absolute certainty what effect a new railway or an agricultural co-operative will have on a nation's social structure. There is not a politician who has not seen one or other of his policies have exactly the opposite effect to what he intended. There is even such a thing as a "fruitful misunderstanding". Take the feudal ruler who regards his lands and his subjects as his family property. If oil strikes have made him rich he will build schools to educate good citizens, but by raising the standard of education he is unwittingly creating the basis for social change.

Can such effects be planned? Social change does not automatically take place as desired. Any number of examples could be given of how large-scale economic and technical projects have tended to harden rather than loosen social structures. There are not only fruitful but also fruitless misunderstandings. What should those people do who were brought out of the bush to help build a large aluminium works which, when completed, needed only a few specialists? Thousands of them do not return to the bush but, having been alienated from their way of life, move to the nearest large towns to swell the numbers of the unemployed proletariat. A paper factory which makes rational use of underwood and can also sell its products presents quite a different picture when we follow what happens to its waste paper. In one African country the waste from one such plant robbed many small fishermen of their living. The fish left the polluted estuary and the small fishing boats were not seaworthy enough to follow them. The ones who benefited from this situation were a fishing company with bigger boats.

Positive concomitants of social change must be planned and directed, adverse ones recognised in good time and prevented. If self-help has come to be regarded as the most important aim of development aid then there is no room for isolated capital aid or technical assistance projects. They can only be considered in connection with social measures. Where jobs in industry are provided, housing, schools and a medical service must be built at the same time. One cannot simply introduce a new variety of wheat without asking who will be able to buy the seed and the fertilizer. Credit and sales co-operatives are necessary if the innovation is not primarily going to benefit those who are fairly well off as it is. Planning a dam involves a study of land and water rights because it depends on this whom the water is going to benefit.

In some cases the social system has become so rigid that it is hardly possible to implement any useful development aid projects. If the members of a certain caste or race cannot find jobs there is no point in training them, even if it is the declared aim of a technical school to integrate them into the community. Training centres should not be established until it is certain that the pupils will later have jobs to go to. Projects specifically aimed at helping those in the poorest sections of the community (social structure aid) cannot make any headway alone, unlike capital aid and technical assistance measures, most of which were designed to meet a particular need and only then were the people considered. With social structure projects it is the people who come first and it is of crucial importance to have a local partner who can appeal to and mobilise them. Yet social change without sensible economic measures is bound to fail. Some projects have had no effect because they have not lived up to the expectations they aroused. Successful attempts to change the outlook of the people always raise their expectations.

Development policy always has some effect on social conditions whether that is the aim or not. Everything depends on recognising these effects—wherever possible —in advance and on guiding them in such a way that they meet the basic needs of the people. For this, too, the combination of different types of project, the transition from the individual project to the programme, has become indispensable. Take, for instance, Ghana's development plan, one aim of which is to reduce the income gap as between urban and rural workers. This may be an end itself but it is an equally good means of halting the drift from the land. Thus the Ghanaian Government propose to invest more in agriculture and rural development.

We have worked out a programme for the development of two rural districts in harmony with Ghana's plan and her requests for aid. Provision has been made for a building depot for road construction in the relatively small coastal region, the promotion of coastal fishing, a poultry breeding project, a medical station and an apprentice workshop. In the vast Northern Region rice-growing and its processing in rice mills will be promoted. In addition, there will be projects for improving public health services and water supply systems. Industrial projects, such as wood-processing establishments to make better use of the forests will also affect the rural districts.

The incorporation of all these projects into Ghana's development plan will ensure that they do not end up in "ruins", for the very fact that the projects complement each other and at the same time fit into a wider concept justifies the hope that they will serve their purpose : to improve living conditions on the land. This becomes even more apparent where international organisations are involved. The World Bank and the United Nations Development Programme also have to make allowance for the interests and susceptibilities of the government concerned, but they cannot so easily be accused of wanting to interfere in the affairs of one country for the benefit of another.

"Concerted dialogue on the spot", the discussion of development plans by the developing countries, the international organisations and the industrial countries involved, opens up a new opportunity. If the local representative of the UNDP is able and willing to raise the question of social structure then it will not fail to have an effect. And he will not only be able to refer to the strategy adopted by the United Nations on 24 April 1970 but also to the resolution of UNESCO and the ILO. One might dispute whether the United Nations has achieved very much in the way of directly safeguarding peace, which is the purpose for which it was established, but in the field of development aid, for which it certainly was not established, it could still have a great future.

6. In Our Own Country

The fact that it is not enough to change developing countries but that the industrial countries must adapt themselves to a new division of labour has meanwhile become a truism. All the same, it is a long way from a truism to reality. It is neither a matter of course nor insignificant that the Cabinet decision of 11 February 1971 contains the sentence : "Structural changes caused by the increased integration of the developing countries into the international division of labour should not be hindered. Rather they should, if necessary, be encouraged through appropriate structural policy measures".

121

But nobody should succumb to the illusion that this completes the job. The negotiations on customs preferences have shown how cautiously governments have to operate where economic adjustments and therefore jobs are involved. Our own country will be one of the arenas where the struggle to achieve an effective development policy in this decade will be decided.

To give an example : in the Federal Republic of Germany labour is scarcer than capital, whereas in the developing countries it is just the opposite. In the first case the answer is to import foreign labour; in the other, German private investment. In 1971 there were more than two million foreign workers in Germany, most of them from European developing countries or North African Mediterranean countries. Now there is also a gradual flow of labour from distant developing countries. These workers are brought to Germany because without them many conveyor belts would be idle, our refuse disposal systems would break down, and our hospitals would be chronically understaffed. Foreign workers are good business for us. As only the healthiest among them are recruited, they spend less time off sick than their German colleagues. They pay the same taxes but they make less use of public services and facilities such as schools and roads. Without their contributions old-age pensions would be smaller or our own contributions would be bigger.

The governments of the countries concerned encourage the migration of workers to the Federal Republic of Germany. They are plagued with unemployment, so that the departure of the jobless gives them at least a temporary breathing space. In addition, the savings of hard currency which foreign workers send home eases the balance of payments difficulties of their native countries. But on closer study the situation is not so favourable. In many cases it is not the unemployed who leave but workers who are urgently needed at home. Tens of thousands of people who have received a technical training, as well as other specialists, come from each of these countries to work in the Federal Republic, and even those who have not had the benefit of a long period of formal schooling are among the most mobile and enterprising groups who could also help to modernise their native countries. Attempts by governments to prevent skilled workers from being enticed away have met with only limited success. On the other hand, the number of those who have received vocational training in the Federal Republic is in most branches extremely small. True, foreign workers learn to cope with industrial production methods and our way of life, but they also grow accustomed to modern working conditions and high wages. This does not make it any easier to re-integrate them in their native countries in such a way as to meet both their own needs and those of the national economy. In the same way that a company's decision to invest in a developing country is based on the conditions prevailing in its own country, foreign workers are brought to Germany to meet the requirements of German industry. It is not a question of development policy but of profitability. We are only now gradually realising that the 400,000 Turks working in Germany mean something in terms of Turkey's development.

In order to facilitate the re-integration of some of these workers into the Turkish economy so that their experience will benefit their native country, the Federal Government has introduced a number of promotional measures. Since June 1971, Turkish skilled workers who want to return home can take a nine-month course of training in Nuremberg leading to a master's certificate (mechanical engineering, motor mechanics, electrical engineering). Afterwards they receive their practical training in Turkey. A similar course started in Cologne last autumn and about 150 Turks will be benefiting from this scheme. The best of them will receive loans from the Federal Government to help them establish their own small businesses, especially in the service industries.

They will be expected to meet part of the investment cost from their own savings. The others will be helped by Turkish agencies to find jobs in Turkish industry.

In Turkey 50 new repair shops, especially for agricultural machinery or electrical services, would be a tangible help. The success of these training programmes will depend on the effect they have in the developing countries. However, the numbers alone show that such a programme, even if it were extended to other countries, will not solve the foreign labour problem in the Federal Republic of Germany. Of the Turkish contingent, 16 to 20 per cent are skilled workers and only they qualify for further training. Moreover, the Federal Government's re-integration programme can only take a small percentage of these even.

Development aid has thus created a model which should induce industrial and social groups to copy. The training of most foreign workers is very inadequate but only with training will their employment in the Federal Republic make any sense in terms of development policy. There is a surplus of unskilled workers in the sending countries and if we want long term co-operation with them our own public and private employers will have to meet their requirements of skilled workers by training rather than recruiting them. This will not alter the fact that even then a large proportion of the foreign workers will have to carry on doing unskilled jobs which Germans will not do, but it will be an encouragement to the sending country, which seems to make this situation more bearable.

VI The Knowledge, the Will, the Ability

1. PUBLIC OPINION

I WOULD not be surprised if it were on the tip of the reader's tongue to say: That's all well and good. You are taking great pains and much of what you are doing makes good sense. You concern yourselves about the right points of departure for your aid, about the best instruments for implementing your programmes, and other tasks, and they are even plausible. Perhaps you really do have a well thought-out concept. But is that enough? Can you guarantee that in ten or twenty years time we shall be over the worst part? What is the relationship, or better the lack of it, between the task in hand and the means available? Is there not a tremendous gap between what is necessary and what is actually done?

The gap between what ought to be done and what is possible and can be pushed through is one of the most distressing experiences of all in the field of development policy. Jan Tinbergen, Chairman of the United Nations Committee on Development Planning, addressing a conference of the Socialist International in Helsinki in May 1971, spoke of the great gulf between what experts consider to be absolutely essential and what politicians actually achieve. Every word he said was perfectly true, I told him, but there was still another gap which was just as agonising as the first—that, between what politicians appreciate is necessary and what they can do.

Tinbergen appealed to national governments on the ground that it was there that the real power still lay.

I replied that ever since I had been concerned with development aid I had felt whenever trying to localise power just as I had in my childhood when I wanted to know where heaven and earth met. Looking out from our house I had seen with my own two eyes that they came together at a certain range of hills. Filled with excitement, I walked over there with my father, but then came the great disappointment: heaven and earth did not touch each other there—nor, as I was soon to learn, anywhere else. Where lies the power to translate development policy concepts into action? Tinbergen was right, of course, governments can do a great deal, and he himself feels that the Federal Government's concept compares favourably with others, but no government can do more than public opinion permits. It can be a few steps ahead of public opinion—and that I think is the case in the Federal Republic of Germany—but it cannot take action without consulting it, or against its will.

It is not true that most Germans are against development aid. On the contrary, a clear majority are in favour of it. Only one quarter of the population, mostly older people, are decidely against it. But the advocates, too, start to hesitate when their attention is drawn to things that need doing in their own country (though in this respect some people have fantastic notions; they seriously believe that money saved by reducing development aid could be used to finance reforms at home). "One" is not against development aid—but not so very much for it either. This is especially true in government and parliamentary circles. Hardly any politician will say he is against development aid. Would that not, after all, be contrary to all party manifestos (with the exception of the National Democratic Party)? But there are many who hedge with a "Yes, but"—the "but" often sounding more convincing than the "Yes". It is not the done thing to be against development aid, but nor is it good to be too much in favour of it for somebody might interpret this as a lack of realism and pragmatism.

Where does this attitude stem from? Could the mass media do anything to change it? Probably, if they were to change themselves. Who, then, is going to inform the public if the journalists in the Federal Republic who know anything about development policy can be counted on the fingers of two hands? Much information and many reports on development aid get no further than the editor's desk because the paper has nobody who can assess their importance. Press conferences without handouts often lead to grotesque reporting, not out of malice but because the journalist who is otherwise capable and normally deals efficiently with economic or foreign affairs can handle development aid statistics no better than information on bilateral and multilateral co-ordination. Who among our television editors has ever been asked to read the Pearson Report, let alone the Jackson Report on United Nations development aid organisations?

When the Federal Government put forward its Development Policy Concept in February 1971 the papers gave it coverage next day in the middle pages only—and there in two columns at the most. When, two months later, acting in a different capacity, I announced the results of the work of a commission appointed to study the question of tax reform they made sprawling headlines. Naturally, there is a good reason for this—readers and television audiences are just not interested! A big illustrated magazine would think twice about presenting its readers with pictures of a technical school. And a provincial paper which printed a report about a new fertilizer factory on the front page would soon be outstripped by its rivals. Or do they only think this because they have not yet realised that in this field, too, the "human touch" is at least as easy to find as in the latest scandal in the world of sport?

Here again we have a vicious circle. Because the mass media provide only little information people know alarmingly little, and they do not provide enough information because their public think other things are more important. The Third World has but little time. And we have little time for the Third World. There is yet another difficulty on top of this : If "dog bites man" is not news but "man bites dog" certainly is, then ninety-eight successful development aid projects are of no news value, but the two that went wrong are. This manner of communicating news may not have any harmful effect on social affairs or tax policy, for nobody would do away with old age pensions because of an irregularity on the part of an insurance authority, nor would they want to close all tax offices because of a bad-mannered clerk. But it is different when it comes to development aid. If it is true that our hard-earned money is used to buy golden bath-tubs or that African chiefs batten on it—then what is the point of it all? As long as German agricultural experts in India can transform a hunger region in India one and a half times the size of the Saarland in Germany into an area of surplus without the German public taking note of it, then legends like the one about the golden bed become dangerous.

This all gives rise to the question why does the government, in other words the Federal Ministry for Economic Co-operation, not intensify its public relations work? It is in fact doing a lot already. It runs an information service, organises exhibitions, supplies material to schools and youth organisations, discusses problems with education ministers and the publishers of textbooks, brings out brochures, some appealing to a narrow, others to a wider public, sponsors films, invites journalists to tour projects, and does its best to stimulate interest in development policy among television corporations. But all this is not enough, particularly as public opinion polls have shown that the Germans think more of development aid the more they know about it, and less of it the vaguer their ideas are. So in this respect any information is publicity.

Publicity for development aid was a fairly simple

undertaking as long as it was only a matter of convincing those who refused to appreciate what all this meant to ourselves. The public were told that the people in the Third World would be able to buy more from us the richer they became—which is not incorrect. And they were shown how good it is to win friends—again not incorrect. But the more we tried to present development aid as something which directly affected our own interests the more that new form of criticism began to take shape in 1968—the neo-colonialist opposition. And this opposition from the left revelled in all those arguments with which it had been hoped to dispel right-wing prejudice. Look there, they would say, you admit that this is all being put on for the sake of our industry. It is not possible to counteract this criticism with a few phrases for it has its ideological foundation and refers to information, however one-sided and distorted it may be. This criticism must be fought with arguments, not emotions.

2. NEO-COLONIALISM?

If used in the exact sense the word neo-colonialism means that forces are at work trying to conserve or re-establish the dependence and the machinery of exploitation of the colonial era with other, less obvious means. In fact it would be rather surprising if such forces did not exist for, after all, colonialism came to an end only a few years ago and political independence is not synonymous with economic independence. Moreover, dependence exists wherever the weak meet the strong. Let us suppose that there had never been a colonial era, nor contacts between the industrial nations of the north and Africa, Asia and Latin America; and supposing we had only just discovered the Southern hemisphere, the problem of dependence would still exist, quite simply because the technologically more advanced nations are also the stronger economically. We are less dependent on what only the Third World has to offer than it is

129

dependent on what only we can supply. Development policy must start from these facts, but it must also try to rectify the situation. Anybody who denounces the mere fact of dependence as "neo-colonialism" gives a pretentious and explosive name to something quite ordinary.

Nobody can doubt that the Colombian coffee grower must today supply more coffee than he did fifteen years ago if he wants to buy a jeep. But, the German farmer—in both parts of the country—must nowadays also sell more wheat than in 1950 if he wants to buy a tractor. In all parts of the world there is a shift in the price ratio as between industrial products on the one hand and most primary commodities on the other. The fact is that the developing countries suffer the most, though the extent differs from country to country. With raw materials it is entirely a question of demand, even though demand can be manipulated. Thus, for instance, the price of rubber fell by 20 per cent in the sixties whilst Egyptian cotton went up by more than 60 per cent.

The terms of trade do not stem from the malicious policies of a few capitalists (as if Communists paid more for their bananas) but from the constellation of power in world markets.[72] If someone were in a position to decree a 50 per cent increase in the price of, say, cotton, the production of that commodity in the developing countries would be boosted, but so too would the manufacture of synthetic fibres in the industrial countries, so that in the end either the market would collapse or there would be regulatory systems in comparison with which all the follies of the EEC would look like child's play. Where the object is to stabilise prices supply must also be stabilised. The fact that structurally weaker countries must be given special preferences is an entirely different matter.

It is certainly a legacy of the colonial era that many developing countries live from the sale of one product only (e.g. coffee, ground-nuts, bananas, cotton). A country whose fate depends on the price of ground-nuts will never be rid of its troubles. Whatever one says about development aid, it does try to diversify such single product economies—this no one can deny. Its ultimate aim is a new division of labour designed to free more and more developing countries from their role of supplying one raw material, and I know as well as anyone that it comes up against massive obstacles.

When today the rather sweeping charge of neo-colonialism is raised, this is partly a reaction to the equally sweeping notion of development aid. The statistics published by the Development Assistance Committee of the OECD, which is the organisation of non-communist industrial countries, correctly distinguish between official aid and private flows, but in the end it is all added together and rendered in German as *Gesamthilfe* (overall aid). Of course, private flows (these include borrowings by the World Bank in the German capital market worth about $260 million in both 1968 and 1969) are definitely a help to the industry of a developing country, but the (pointless) issue is whether the motive is in fact aid. For this reason German statistics have since 1969 been careful to make a clear distinction between official aid and private flows.

When private flows are mentioned one thinks almost exclusively of private direct investment. At the Congress of Churches in Stuttgart, some participants spoke of our development aid as if it consisted merely of private investment. In fact, of the $16,286 million total flow from the Federal Republic of Germany up to and including 1969, $1,720 million took the form of direct investment while $6,300 million was official aid. This gives a ratio of about 1 : 3.7. Compared with the economic strength of the Federal Republic of Germany (foreign trade worth $64,210 million in 1970) the proportion of private investment is minimal. German private companies have made profits in the region of 8 per cent in the Third

World, some 70 per cent of which is re-invested in the host countries.

These figures alone show that our official aid cannot simply serve as a buttress for private investment. Whereas our technical assistance is concentrated on Africa and our capital aid on Asia, nearly three fifths of our private investment goes to Latin America, and fifty per cent of that to Brazil. Thus the ratio of private investment to official aid up to now has been 1 : 9 in Kenya, 1 : 11 in Turkey, 1 : 23 in Morocco, 1 : 25 in Togo, 1 : 30 in India, 1 : 50 in Pakistan, 1 : 56 in Tunisia and 1 : 72 in Ghana. On the other hand, it is 3 : 1 in Argentina, 3 : 1 in Brazil, 6 : 1 in Mexico and even 7 : 1 in Venezuela. The only country where private and official aid from the Federal Republic are more or less on a par is the Ivory Coast. Private German companies have no intention of allowing their investment decisions to be governed by government policies. This also applies the other way round.

Official aid, which is the main theme of this book, is also likened to neo-colonialism, but only as a general criticism. So far no one has been able to prove to me that a particular project was a means of exploitation (although one or two dubious ones in this respect might be found with a little effort). We are always hearing the argument that a capitalist system cannot by definition pursue anything else but exploitation—but that still needs to be proved. No one has yet been able to show me how far Russian aid differs from ours in its effect. Where the Soviet Union gives loans they have the same interest rates as ours, the difference being that they are granted for shorter periods. If it builds a technical school then it adopts the same approach as ourselves. And sometimes I have the impression that we give more thought to the social consequences of our aid than the Russians.

This brings us to the accusation that our aid tends to consolidate obsolete social structures. That would have to be proved project by project and in odd cases this will probably be true, but the great majority, including technical assistance and capital aid, have in fact a dynamising effect on structures. Only those who believe that the longed-for, saving revolution will be helped by letting the country make do on its own resources will be able to denounce our aid as support for existing social hierarchies. Up to today, however, revolutions have not stemmed from the wretchedly poor illiterates. Where education is improved, where the people unite their efforts in co-operatives, and where industries are built up, this creates the basis for social progress.

3. The Political Scope

I do not regret any discussion of neo-colonialism in so far as it draws attention to the weaknesses of our policies, but I do if it diverts attention from more important problems. Whether we are neo-colonialists or not is determined not so much by facts as by our theoretical points of departure. Whether and to what extent our aid contributions will increase in the next few years means a great deal to the developing country. Whether there is, or can ever be, a society able to provide the developing countries with adequate and ideal assistance is clearly disputable. What interests the developing countries is whether and when we can achieve the United Nations target of 0.7 per cent of the gross national product in the form of official aid, what we can do to reduce their indebtedness, what import policy the EEC will pursue in the seventies, what training our experts receive, the extent to which we incorporate our projects into multilateral programmes, and how the efforts of the industrial and the developing countries can be better co-ordinated. And above all they are interested in whether public opinion will permit us to pursue a generous development policy. Thus the real line of division runs not between those who regard development aid as humanitarian and those who criticise it, but between those who want a better development policy and those who declare that a reasonable development in our community is impossible from the outset.

Today a country's development policy is a fairly true reflection of its attitude. A crisis for the Americans is also a crisis for their development policy. The outward-looking policy of the Swedes is mirrored in the size of their development aid contributions. Every nation has the development policy—and ultimately the development aid ministry also—it deserves. If only two groups speak up in Germany, those who say development aid is a waste of money and those who regard it as neo-colonialism, then this country cannot render the contribution which the nations of the Southern hemisphere expect of it. As long as small active groups eliminate each other in a two-front struggle against sweeping prejudice, constructive development policy will be labour in vain and only too frequently lead to frustration. Only when a critical, knowledgeable public—as in Sweden—make concrete and realistic demands on the government will development policy be given the priority it deserves.

Those who understand, pursue and present development policy in this way will not be able to escape the criticism of those who see in all this a lack of national feeling. Where it is a question of social change they suspect a social conspiracy, if we identify ourselves with the aims of the developing countries they accuse us of having no thought for our fatherland, where ingrained ideologies are to be eliminated they complain of ideologists, and where we refuse favours they lament the lack of realism. None of this would be so bad if it did not narrow the scope which any policy needs. The more elegantly the critics on the left and on the right strike the ball into each other's court, the greater will be the gap between what a politician realises should be done and what he actually can do.

The Pearson Report defines development policy as recognition of the fact that the endeavour to achieve better living conditions is no longer divisible. In other words, aid for the Third World is not a hobby for a few eccentric idealists, not alms-giving to appease uneasy consciences, not a compulsory exercise for bored politicians, and not a means of safeguarding the export trade of industrial countries. Where nothing swings into line, where the unbearable can be calculated without the aid of a computer, aid for the Third World is an ambitious attempt to make life for all on earth more bearable so that it will not become unbearable for all, an investment in the common future because there will be either a common future or no future at all.

Notes

1 See *Der Spiegel*, No. 20, 10 May 1971.
2 See L. J. Lebret, *Dynamique concrète du développement*, Paris 1961.
3 From an unpublished dissertation by E. Eisenlehr, pp. 40–41: "The state also takes steps to ensure a balance between the people and the land: by setting up *mitimaes* (model family groups) people were transferred from densely populated areas so that every national could be given a piece of land for his subsistence."
4 R. F. Behrendt, *Soziale Strategie für Entwicklungsländer*, Frankfurt a.M. 1965, p. 258.
5 Data taken from summarised reports on individual countries published by the Federal Statistical Office.
5a International Labour Office, *Towards full employment. A programme for Colombia*, Geneva 1970.
6 ILO, Geneva 1970, *Towards a World Employment Programme*, p. 32.
7 F. Baade, *Weltweiter Wohlstand*, Oldenburg and Hamburg 1970, p. 9: "... that the biggest reserves of prosperity of the developing countries lie precisely in the millions of people capable of work ...". "Thus those people today living in extreme poverty possess an almost inexhaustible goldmine: hundreds of millions of unproductive but mobilisable workers."
8 Ibid., p. 25.
9 *Der Spiegel*, No. 23/71, p. 29.
10 H. R. Hulett, "Optimum World Population", *Bio Science*, vol. 20, No. 3 (1970).
11 Paul R. Ehrlich, Anne H. Ehrlich, "Population, Resources, Environment", *Issues in Human Ecology*, San Francisco 1970, p. 201.
12 Hermann Kahn, Anthony J. Wiener, *The year 2000. A Framework for Speculation on the next Thirty-Three Years*, London 1968, p. 139.
13 Press and Information Office of the Federal Government, Bulletin No. 65, p. 667.
14 According to the Pearson Report, nineteen countries achieved annual average growth rates of more than 6 per cent of

GNP between 1960 and 1967. Nine of these, including Mexico, Libya and Panama, had a *per capita* income of $500 GNP or more. Only three developing countries with a relatively small *per capita* income ($100–199) also achieved growth rates of over 6 per cent: Thailand, Mauritania and South Korea. See *Partners in Development,* 1969, Annex II, Table 2, p. 360.

15 See W. W. Rostow, *Stages of Economic Growth,* Cambridge 1960.

16 P. and A. Ehrlich, loc. cit., p. 127.

17 Ivan Illich, "Muss die Dritte Welt wie die Erste werden?" in: *Neues Forum,* May 1970, p. 568.

18 Julius K. Nyerere, "Freedom and Socialism". *Uhuru na Ujamaa,* Dar es Salaam 1969, pp. 267–8.

19 Ibid., p. 275.

20 Speech in Salzburg at the Youth and Development Conference, May 1970.

21 Rene Maheu, Director General of UNESCO, in his message for International Education Year 1970.

22 Nyerere, loc. cit., p. 354.

23 E. F. Schumacher, "Industrialisation through Intermediate Technology", in: *Industrialisation in Developing Countries,* edited by Ronald Robinson, Cambridge University Press 1965.

24 Ivan Illich, *Almosen und Folter,* Munich 1970, p. 133.

25 See *Nachrichten für Aussenhandel NfA,* 13 May 1971.

26 *The World Employment Programme,* ILO, Geneva 1969, p. 41.

27 Ibid., pp. 42–5

28 Ibid., p. 41 et seq.

29 Ibid., p. 29 et seq.

30 *The Pearson Report,* p. 58.

31 *Development Assistance—Efforts and Policies of the Members of the Development Assistance Committee,* OECD 1970, p. 128.

32 See G. Myrdal, *Politisches Manifest über die Armut in der Welt,* Frankfurt a.M. 1970, p. 13 et seq.

33 *World Employment Programme,* p. 30.

34 R. Prebisch, *Change and Development,* Washington 1970, p. 28.

35 *World Employment Programme,* p. 45 et seq.

36 Ibid., p. 30.

37 See *Development Assistance,* loc. cit., p. 126 et seq.

38 Estimate of the UN Economic Commission for Latin America in 1960. Quoted by R. Prebisch in *Change and Development,* Washington 1970, p. 112.

39 IBRD-IDA-IFC, *Trends in Developing Countries*, Washington 1970, Table 4.5 and *Annual Report 1970*, loc cit., p. 43.

40 *Trends in Developing Countries*, Table 4.3.

41 See Footnote 40.

42 Ibid., Table 4.4.

43 Calculated according to the IBRD-IDA *Annual Report 1970*, p. 44.

44 *The Pearson Report*, p. 81.

45 Calculated according to the IBRD-IBA *Annual Report 1970*, p. 44.

46 See the *Pearson Report*, pp. 91–2, and *Auswertung der Dokumentation der zweiten Welthandelskonferenz* (1968), No. 1, pp. 25–7, and No. 2, p. 211.

47 Calculated according to *Trends in Developing Countries*, Table 4.1.

48 See Footnote 45.

49 See *Auswertung der Dokumentation der zweiten Welthandelskonferenz*, No. 2, p. 210.

50 Ibid., p. 221.

51 Calculated according to the IBRD-IDA *Annual Report 1970*, pp. 68 and 71.

52 *The Pearson Report*, p. 48.

53 Para. 17 of the UN Strategy Document DDII.

54 *The Pearson Report*, p. 49.

55 See Myrdal's excellent description of the "soft state" in: *Politisches Manifest*, loc. cit., p. 102 et sec.

56 Lindner, in: *Überseerundschau*, May 1971, p. 14.

57 R. F. Mikesell, *The Economics of Foreign Aid*, Chicago 1968, p. 11: "If there are any national economic benefits accruing to aid donors (other than from export credits), they are largely indirect, highly tenuous and of such a long-term nature that their discounted value will almost surely be exceeded by present costs."

58 Of the Federal Republic of Germany's total exports in 1970 ($34,228 million) the greater proportion went to Western industrial countries ($26,918 million) and the socialist countries ($1,475 million); goods exported to the developing countries were worth $5,835 million. Exports to developing countries had increased by 38 per cent since 1965, those to Western industrial countries by 75 per cent, and to state trading countries by as much as 170 per cent (provisional figures).

59 *The Pearson Report*, p. 9.

60 Rudolph A. Peterson, Chairman: US Foreign Assistance in the 1970s: A new approach. Report to the President from

the Task Force on International Development, 4 March 1970.

61 See, for example, R. F. Mikesell, *The Economics of Foreign Aid*, p. 7.

62 "Aid has often been directed at the promotion or financing of exports from developed countries with little relevance to development objectives in the receiving countries." *Pearson Report*, p. 50. The fact that this problem also exists in the multilateral sphere is again illustrated in the *Jackson Report*. In this field certain individual interests of multilateral specialised organisations lead to the selection and implementation of projects which likewise have little to do with the aims of the receiving countries (United Nations, *A Study of the Capacity of the United Nations Development System*, Geneva 1969, vol. II, p. 75).

63 *The Pearson Report*, p. 4.

64 M. E. Bond and F. J. Mathis, "The Disinterest in Foreign Aid: An Appraisal", in: *Kyklos*, 23rd year (1970), No. 3, p. 469.

65 Ibid., p. 448 et seq.

66 *Development Policy Concept of the Federal Republic of Germany for the Second Development Decade*, published by the Federal Ministry for Economic Co-operation, Bonn 1971, 11–12.

67 Ibid., p. 14.

68 Ibid., p. 15.

69 Ibid., pp. 7–8.

70 Ibid., p. 22.

71 Ibid., p. 10.

72 See Myrdal, *Politisches Manifest*, loc. cit. p. 274 et seq.

Selected Literature

Baade, Fritz, Dynamische Weltwirtschaft. Munich 1969; Weltweiter Wohlstand. Oldenburg und Hamburg 1970.

Behrendt, Richard F., Soziale Strategie für Entwicklungsländer. Frankfurt 1965.

Besters, Hans and *Boesch, Ernst* (publ.), Entwicklungspolitik, Handbuch und Lexikon. Stuttgart und Munich 1966.

Bundesministerium für wirtschaftliche Zusammenarbeit (publ.), Entwicklungspolitische Konzeption der Bundesrepublik Deutschland und Internationale Strategie für die Zweite Entwicklungsdekade. Bonn 1971; Strukturdaten der Unterentwicklung, Frankfurt 1971.

Bundesstelle für Aussenhandelsinformation, Die Konferenz der Gruppe der 77 und die Charta von Algier. Prepared and translated by M. Timmler. Cologne 1968.

Chesneaur. Jean, Geschichte Ost- und Südostasiens im 19 und 20. Jahrhundert. Cologne 1969.

Dankwerts, Dankwart, Entwicklungshilfe als imperialistische Politik. Dortmund 1968.

Dennert, Jürgen, Entwicklungshilfe, geplant oder verwaltet? Bielefeld 1968.

Offene Welt No. 99/100, Die Dritte Welt als Bildungsaufgabe, Cologne and Opladen 1969.

Dumont, René, L'Afrique Noire est mal partie. 1967.

Duve, Freimut, Der Rassenkrieg findet nicht statt. Entwicklungspolitik zwischen Angst und Armut. Düsseldorf and Vienna 1971.

Ehrlich, Paul R. and *Anne H.,* Population, Resources, Environment. Issues in Human Ecology, San Francisco 1970.

Eisenlohr, Edda, Agrarreform in Equador im entwicklungspolitischen Kräftespiel. Dortmund 1969.

EKD (Sozialwissenschaftl. Institut) und Brot für die Welt, Entwicklungspolitische Dokumente. Wuppertal-Barmen 1970.

Engelbrecht. Helga (ed.), Materialien zur Entwicklungshilfekritik, Bonn DSE 1969.

Evangelischer Akademikertag, Entwicklungspolitik zwischen Geschäft und Gewissen. Sixth Evangelical Academic Congress, 2–4 October 1970 in Tübingen. Dokumentation.

Eppler, Erhard, Entwicklungspolitik und Eigeninteressen. In:

Europa-Archiv, Series 6, 1971. Spannungsfelder. Beiträge zur Politik unserer Zeit. Stuttgart 1969.

Fanon Frantz, Die Verdammten dieser Erde, Frankfurt 1966.

Food and Agriculture Organization of the United Nations (FAO), Provisional Indicative World Plan for Agricultural Development. A Synthesis and Analysis of Factors Relevant to World, Regional and National Agricultural Development, vol. 2, Rome 1960. The State of Food and Agriculture 1970. Rome 1970.

Fohrbeck, Wiesand Zahar, Heile Welt—Dritte Welt (results of textbook analysis). Opladen 1971.

Fritsch, Bruno (ed.), Entwicklungsländer. Neue Wissenschaftliche Bibliothek. Cologne-Berlin 1968.

Fritsch, Bruno, Die Vierte Welt. Stuttgart 1970.

Gatz, W., Auswertung der Dokumentation der zweiten Welthandelskonferenz (1968), 3 vols. Series published by the Federal Ministry for Economic Co-operation. Stuttgart 1970.

Heinrichs, Jürgen (ed.), Welternährungskrise oder ist eine Hungerkatastrophe unausweichlich? rororo aktuell. Reinbek 1968.

Holzer, Werner, 26mal Afrika. Munich 1967.

Horlemann, Jürgen, Modelle der kolonialen Konterrevolution, Frankfurt 1968.

Illich, Ivan D., Almosen und Folter. Verfehlter Fortschritt in Lateinamerika. Munich 1970.

Institut für Sozialforschung an der Johann-Wolfgang-Goethe-Universität, Kritische Analyse von Schulbüchern zur Darstellung der Probleme der Entwicklungsländer und ihrer Positionen in internationalen Beziehungen, Frankfurt 1970.

International Labour Office (ILO), The World Employment Programme. Geneva 1969.

International Labour Organization (ILO), Towards Full Employment—An Employment Strategy for Colombia. ILO, Geneva 1970.

International Strategy for the Second UN Development Decade DDII.

Jesus, Carolina Maria de, Tagebuch der Armut. Aufzeichnungen einer brasilianischen Negerin. Frankfurt 1968.

Kahn, Hermann, Wiener, Anthony J., The Year 2000. A Framework for Speculation on the Next Thirty-Three Years. Macmillan, London-New York 1968.

Klingener, K. H., Meyer J. and *Seul, D.*, Die Zweite Entwicklungsdekade der Vereinten Nationen—Konzept und Kritik einer globalen Entwicklungsstrategie. Düsseldorf 1971.

Lefringhausen, Klaus, Merz, Friedhelm, Das Zweite Entwicklungsjahrzehnt 1970 bis 1980. Wuppertal-Barmen 1970.

Lerner, Daniel, The Passing of Traditional Society. Modernizing the Middle East. Free Press Paperback Edition. New York 1965.

Lewis, Oscar, The Children of Sanchez, self-portrait of a Mexican family, New York 1961.

Lüning, Hildegard (ed.), Mit Maschinengewehr und Kreuz oder wie kann das Christentum überleben? rororo aktuell. Hamburg 1971.

Mao Tse-Tung, Theorie des Guerilla-Krieges, Reinbek 1966.

Massachusetts Institute of Technology, Man's impact on the global environment. MIT Press 1970.

Meueler Erhard, Soziale Gerechtigkeit. Einführung in die Entwicklungsproblematik am Beispiel Brasiliens und der Bundesrepublik Deutschland. Textbuch und Didaktisches Beiheft. Düsseldorf 1971.

Michanek, Ernst, The World Development Plan. A Swedish Perspective. Stockholm 1971.

Myrdal, Gunnar, Politisches Manifest über die Armut in der Welt. Frankfurt 1970. Asian Drama. 3 vols., London 1968.

Nyerere, Julius K., Freedom and Socialism. Uhuru na Ujamaa. Oxford University Press, Dar es Salaam 1969.

Organization for Economic Co-operation and Development (OECD), Development Assistance, Efforts and Policies of the members of the Development Assistance Committee. Paris 1970.

Pearson, L. et al., Partners in Development. Report of the Commission on International Development. Praeger, New York. Washington. London 1969.

Paul VI., Populorum Progressio. Über den Fortschritt der Völker. Kommentar und Einführung von H. Krauss S. J. Herder-Bücherei. Freiburg 1970.

Prebisch, Raúl, Change and Development—Latin America's Great Task—Interamerican Development Bank. Washington 1970.

Rostow, Walt Whitmann, Stages of Economic Growth, Cambridge 1960.

Scheel, Walter, Konturen einer neuen Welt. Düsseldorf 1965.

Schumacher, E. F., Technische Zwischenlösungen. In: Stichwörter zur Entwicklungshilfe. Nuremberg 1970.

Steinbuch, Karl, Programm 2000. Stuttgart 1970.

Turnham, D., The Employment Problem in Less Developed Countries—A Review of Evidence, OECD, Paris 1970.

United Nations. A Study of the Capacity of the United Nations Development System. (Jackson Report). 2 vols. UN Geneva 1969.

Wischnewski, Hans Jürgen, Nord-Süd-Konflikt. Beiträge zur Entwicklungspolitik. Hanover 1968.
World Bank, International Development Association, Annual Report 1970. Washington 1970. Trends in Developing Countries. Washington 1970.

PERIODICALS AND SERIES

Afrika Heute, published by the German Africa Association.
Aktion Entwicklungshilfe, Jugenddienst Verlag/Verlag Haus Altenberg, edited by Baumgärtner, S., Falkenstörfer, H., Lefringhausen K.
Blätter des iz3w, published by Informationzentrum Dritte Welt.
DED-Brief, Information des Deutschen Entwicklungsdienstes, published by the German Volunteer Service (DED), Bonn-Bad Godesberg.
Entwicklungspolitik, Materialien, published by the Federal Ministry for Economic Co-operation.
Entwicklungspolitik, Spiegel der Presse, published by the Federal Ministry for Economic Co-operation.
Entwicklung und Zusammenarbeit, published by the German Foundation for Developing Countries, Bonn.
epd-Entwicklungspolitik, published by the Information Branch, Evangelical Press Service, Frankfurt.
Far Eastern Economic Review, Hongkong.
Inter Economics, Monthly Review of International Trade and Development. Verlag Weltarchiv GmbH, Hamburg.
Internationales Afrika-Forum, monthly edn., Munich.
Internationales Asien-Forum, quarterly edn., Munich.
Landwirt im Ausland, published by DLG, DSE und GAWI.
Marchés tropicaux et méditerranéens, Paris. Edited by Moreux, René.
Schriften der Kübel-Stiftung, published by the Kübel Foundation, Bensheim-Auerbach.
Schule und Dritte Welt, Texte und Materialien—Anregungen für den Unterricht, published by the Federal Ministry for Economic Co-operation.
Series published by the Federal Ministry for Economic Co-operation, Ernst Klett Verlag.
Quarterly Reports on the Problems of Developing Countries, published by the Research Institute of the Friedrich Ebert Foundation.